TOOLS FOR CONVIVIALITY

TOOLS FOR CONVIVIALITY

IVAN ILLICH

HARPER COLOPHON BOOKS
Harper & Row, Publishers
New York, Cambridge, Hagerstown, Philadelphia, San Francisco
London, Mexico City, São Paulo, Sydney

A hardcover edition of this book is published by Harper & Row, Publishers, Inc. Portions of this book appeared in the March-April 1973 issue of *Social Policy Magazine*. Other portions appeared in *Saturday Review of Education* of May 1973.

This Harper Colophon paperback edition is a reprint of Volume 47 of the World Perspectives Series, which is planned and edited by Ruth Nanda Anshen. Dr. Anshen's Epilogue appears on page 124.

First HARPER COLOPHON edition published 1980.

ISBN: 0-06-090743-6

80 81 82 83 84 10 9 8 7 6 5 4 3 2 1

Contents

Acknowledgments

The multidimensional analysis of ceilings for industrial growth was first formulated in a Spanish document coauthored by Valentina Borremans and myself and submitted as a guideline for a meeting of two dozen Chilean socialists and other Latin Americans at CIDOC (the Center for Intercultural Documentation) in Cuernavaca, Mexico. The next version was presented at the Zeno Symposium organized by Professor Richard Wollheim in Cyprus. It was published in *Esprit*, Paris, March 1972, with criticisms by Th. Adam, Pierre Caussat, J. P. Chevenement, Paul Fraisse, Yves Goussault, Pierre Kende, J. W. Lapierre, Michel Panoff, Henri Pequignot, Jean Marie Domenach, and Paul Thibaud. A third version served me and my deceased friend Greer Taylor as the basis for our participation in the Canadian Conference on the Law in January 1972 in Ottawa. Comments by David Weisstub, Nils Christie, Allen M. Linden, J. G. Castel, H. W. Arthurs, José Antonio Viera-Gallo, J. C. Smith, and Bonaventura de Sousa Santos, and other critical papers by jurists, will be published in mid-1973 in Toronto. During the summer of 1972, participants in my CIDOC seminar contributed very helpful papers. I'm especially grateful for the assistance of John Bradley, John Brewer, José María and Veronica Bulnes, Martin Cohen, Irene Curbelo de Diaz, Dennis Detzel, Joseph Fitzpatrick, Amnon Goldworth, Conrad Johnson, Hartmut von Hentig, John MacKnight, Michael Maccoby, Leslie Marcus, Francisco Miró Quesada, Marie-Noëlle Monteil, William Ophuls, Marta H. Reed, Everett Reimer, Francisco Varela, Etienne Verne, Jacques Vidal and German Zabala. Dennis Sullivan has patiently and critically assisted me in editing the final version. After I had delivered this manuscript to the publisher, I received valuable suggestions from J. P. Naik and his friends in India. These have seeped into the text to the extent this can happen in the correction of proofs. Second only to Valentina Borremans and Greer Taylor, Heinz von Foerster, Erich Fromm, Hermann Schwember and Abrahán Diaz Gonzales have exerted the most decisive influence on the formulation of my ideas.

Introduction

During the next several years I intend to work on an epilogue to the industrial age. I want to trace the changes in language, myth, ritual, and law which took place in the current epoch of packaging and of schooling. I want to describe the fading monopoly of the industrial mode of production and the vanishing of the industrially generated professions this mode of production serves.

Above all I want to show that two-thirds of mankind still can avoid passing through the industrial age, by choosing right now a postindustrial balance in their mode of production which the hyperindustrial nations will be forced to adopt as an alternative to chaos. To prepare for this task I submit this essay for critical comment.

In its present form this book is the result of conversations at CIDOC in Cuernavaca during the summer of 1972. Participants in my seminar will recognize their ideas, and often their words. I ask my collaborators to accept my sincere thanks, especially for their written contributions.

This essay has become too long to appear as an article and too intricate to be read in several installments. It is a progress report. I respectfully thank Ruth Nanda Anshen for issuing this tract as a volume, in *World Perspectives*, published by Harper & Row.

For several years at CIDOC in Cuernavaca we have conducted critical research on the monopoly of the industrial mode of production and have tried to define conceptually alternative modes that would fit a postindustrial age. During the late sixties this research centered on educational devices. By 1970 we had found that:

1. Universal education through compulsory schooling is not possible.
2. Alternative devices for the production and marketing of mass education are technically more feasible and ethically less tolerable than compulsory graded schools. Such new educational arrangements are now on the verge of replacing traditional school systems in rich and in poor countries. They are potentially more effective in the conditioning of job-holders and consumers in an industrial economy. They are therefore more attractive for the management of present societies, more seductive for the people, and insidiously destructive of fundamental values.
3. A society committed to high levels of shared learning and critical personal intercourse must set pedagogical limits on industrial growth.

I have published the results of this research in a previous volume of *World Perspectives,* entitled *Deschooling Society.* I clarified some of the points left ill defined in that book by writing an article published in the *Saturday Review* of April 19, 1971.

Our analysis of schooling has led us to recognize the mass production of education as a paradigm for other industrial enterprises, each producing a service commodity, each organized as a public utility, and each defining its output as a basic necessity. At first our attention was drawn to the compulsory insurance of professional health care, and to systems of public transport, which tend to become compulsory once traffic rolls above a certain speed. We found that the industrialization of any service agency leads to destructive side effects analogous to the unwanted secondary results well known from the overproduction of goods. We had to face a set of limits to growth in the service sector of any society as inescapable as the limits inherent in the industrial produc-

tion of artifacts. We concluded that a set of limits to industrial growth is well formulated only if these limits apply
both to goods and to services which are produced in an industrial mode. So we set out to clarify these limits.

I here submit the concept of a multidimensional balance
of human life which can serve as a framework for evaluating
man's relation to his tools. In each of several dimensions of
this balance it is possible to identify a natural scale. When
an enterprise grows beyond a certain point on this scale, it
first frustrates the end for which it was originally designed,
and then rapidly becomes a threat to society itself. These
scales must be identified and the parameters of human endeavors within which human life remains viable must be
explored.

Society can be destroyed when further growth of mass production renders the milieu hostile, when it extinguishes the
free use of the natural abilities of society's members, when
it isolates people from each other and locks them into a
man-made shell, when it undermines the texture of community by promoting extreme social polarization and splinter-
ing specialization, or when cancerous acceleration enforces
social change at a rate that rules out legal, cultural, and political precedents as formal guidelines to present behavior.
Corporate endeavors which thus threaten society cannot be
tolerated. At this point it becomes irrelevant whether an enterprise is nominally owned by individuals, corporations, or
the state, because no form of management can make such
fundamental destruction serve a social purpose.

Our present ideologies are useful to clarify the contradictions which appear in a society which relies on the capitalist
control of industrial production; they do not, however, provide the necessary framework for analyzing the crisis in the
industrial mode of production itself. I hope that one day a
general theory of industrialization will be stated with preci-
sion, that it will be formulated in terms compelling enough
to withstand the test of criticism. Its concepts ought to provide a common language for people in opposing parties who
need to engage in the assessment of social programs or tech-

nologies, and who want to restrain the power of man's tools
when they tend to overwhelm man and his goals. Such a
theory should help people invert the present structure of
major institutions. I hope that this essay will enhance the
formulation of such a theory.

It is now difficult to imagine a modern society in which
industrial growth is balanced and kept in check by several
complementary, distinct, and equally scientific modes of production. Our vision of the possible and the feasible is so restricted by industrial expectations that any alternative to
more mass production sounds like a return to past oppression or like a Utopian design for noble savages. In fact,
however, the vision of new possibilities requires only the
recognition that scientific discoveries can be used in at least
two opposite ways. The first leads to specialization of functions, institutionalization of values and centralization of
power and turns people into the accessories of bureaucracies
or machines. The second enlarges the range of each person's
competence, control, and initiative, limited only by other
individuals' claims to an equal range of power and freedom.

To formulate a theory about a future society both very
modern and not dominated by industry, it will be necessary
to recognize natural scales and limits. We must come to admit that only within limits can machines take the place of
slaves; beyond these limits they lead to a new kind of serfdom. Only within limits can education fit people into a man-
made environment: beyond these limits lies the universal
schoolhouse, hospital ward, or prison. Only within limits
ought politics to be concerned with the distribution of
maximum industrial outputs, rather than with equal inputs
of either energy or information. Once these limits are recognized, it becomes possible to articulate the triadic relationship between persons, tools, and a new collectivity. *Such a
society, in which modern technologies serve politically interrelated individuals rather than managers, I will call "convivial."*

After many doubts, and against the advice of friends
whom I respect, *I have chosen "convivial" as a technical*

term to designate a modern society of responsibly limited tools. In part this choice was conditioned by the desire to continue a discourse which had started with its Spanish cognate. The French cognate has been given technical meaning (for the kitchen) by Brillat-Savarin in his *Physiology of Taste: Meditations on Transcendental Gastronomy.* This specialized use of the term in French might explain why it has already proven effective in the unmistakably different and equally specialized context in which it will appear in this essay. I am aware that in English "convivial" now seeks the company of tipsy jollyness, which is distinct from that indicated by the OED and opposite to the austere meaning of modern *"eutrapelia,"* which I intend. By applying the term "convivial" to tools rather than to people, I hope to forestall confusion.

"Austerity," which says something about people, has also been degraded and has acquired a bitter taste, while for Aristotle or Aquinas it marked the foundation of friendship. In the *Summa Theologica,* II, II, in the 186th question, article 5, Thomas deals with disciplined and creative playfulness. In his third response he defines "austerity" as a virtue which does not exclude all enjoyments, but only those which are distracting from or destructive of personal relatedness. For Thomas "austerity" is a complementary part of a more embracing virtue, which he calls friendship or joyfulness. It is the fruit of an apprehension that things or tools could destroy rather than enhance *eutrapelia* (or graceful playfulness) in personal relations.*

---

* Hugo Rahner, *Man at Play,* New York, 1972.

I

Two Watersheds

The year 1913 marks a watershed in the history of modern medicine. Around that year a patient began to have more than a fifty-fifty chance that a graduate of a medical school would provide him with a specifically effective treatment (if, of course, he was suffering from one of the standard diseases recognized by the medical science of the time). Many shamans and herb doctors familiar with local diseases and remedies and trusted by their clients had always had equal or better results.

Since then medicine has gone on to define what constitutes disease and its treatment. The Westernized public learned to demand effective medical practice as defined by the progress of medical science. For the first time in history doctors could measure their efficiency against scales which they themselves had devised. This progress was due to a new perspective of the origins of some ancient scourges; water could be purified and infant mortality lowered; rat control could disarm the plague; treponemas could be made visible under the microscope and Salvarsan could eliminate them with statistically defined risks of poisoning the patient; syphilis could be avoided, or recognized and cured by rather simple procedures; diabetes could be diagnosed and self-treatment with insulin could prolong the life of the patient. Paradoxically, the simpler the tools became, the more the medical profession insisted on a monopoly of their application, the longer became the training demanded before a medicine man was initiated into the legitimate use of the simplest tool, and the more the entire population felt dependent on the doctor. Hygiene turned from being a virtue into a professionally organized ritual at the altar of a science.

Infant mortality was lowered, common forms of infection were prevented or treated, some forms of crisis intervention became quite effective. The spectacular decline in mortality and morbidity was due to changes in sanitation, agriculture, marketing, and general attitudes toward life. But though these changes were sometimes influenced by the attention that engineers paid to new facts discovered by medical science, they could only occasionally be ascribed to the intervention of doctors.

Indirectly, industrialization profited from the new effectiveness attributed to medicine; work attendance was raised, and with it the claim to efficiency on the job. The destructiveness of new tools was hidden from public view by new techniques of providing spectacular treatments for those who fell victims to industrial violence such as the speed of cars, tension on the job, and poisons in the environment.

The sickening side effects of modern medicine became obvious after World War II, but doctors needed time to diagnose drug-resistant microbes or genetic damage caused by prenatal X-rays as new epidemics. The claim made by George Bernard Shaw a generation earlier, that doctors had ceased to be healers and were assuming control over the patient's entire life, could still be regarded as a caricature. Only in the mid-fifties did it become evident that medicine had passed a second watershed and had itself created new kinds of disease.

Foremost among iatrogenic (doctor-induced) diseases was the pretense of doctors that they provided their clients with superior health. First, social planners and doctors became its victims. Soon this epidemic aberration spread to society at large. Then, during the last fifteen years, professional medicine became a major threat to health. Huge amounts of money were spent to stem immeasurable damage caused by medical treatments. The cost of healing was dwarfed by the cost of extending sick life; more people

survived longer months with their lives hanging on a
plastic tube, imprisoned in iron lungs, or hooked onto kid-
ney machines. New sickness was defined and institutionalized; the cost of enabling people to survive in unhealthy
cities and in sickening jobs sky-rocketed. The monopoly
of the medical profession was extended over an increasing
range of everyday occurrences in every man's life.

The exclusion of mothers, aunts, and other nonpro-
fessionals from the care of their pregnant, abnormal, hurt,
sick, or dying relatives and friends resulted in new demands
for medical services at a much faster rate than the medical
establishment could deliver. As the value of *services* rose, it
became almost impossible for people to *care*. Simultaneously, more conditions were defined as needing treatment
by creating new specializations or paraprofessions to keep
the tools under the control of the guild.

At the time of the second watershed, preservation of the
sick life of medically dependent people in an unhealthy environment became the principal business of the medical
profession. Costly prevention and costly treatment became
increasingly the privilege of those individuals who through
previous consumption of medical services had established
a claim to more of it. Access to specialists, prestige hospitals, and life-machines goes preferentially to those people who live in large cities, where the cost of basic disease
prevention, as of water treatment and pollution control,
is already exceptionally high. The higher the per capita
cost of prevention, the higher, paradoxically, became the
per capita cost of treatment. The prior consumption of
costly prevention and treatment establishes a claim for
even more extraordinary care. Like the modern school
system, hospital-based health care fits the principle that
those who have will receive even more and those who have
not will be taken for the little that they have. In schooling
this means that high consumers of education will get post-
doctoral grants, while dropouts learn that they have failed.
In medicine the same principle assures that suffering will

increase with increased medical care; the rich will be given more treatment for iatrogenic diseases and the poor will just suffer from them.

After this second turning point, the unwanted hygienic by-products of medicine began to affect entire populations rather than just individual men. In rich countries medicine began to sustain the middle-aged until they became decrepit and needed more doctors and increasingly complex medical tools. In poor countries, thanks to modern medicine, a larger percentage of children began to survive into adolescence and more women survived more pregnancies. Populations increased beyond the capacities of their environments and the restraints and efficiencies of their cultures to nurture them. Western doctors abused drugs for the treatment of diseases with which native populations had learned to live. As a result they bred new strains of disease with which modern treatment, natural immunity, and traditional culture could not cope. On a world-wide scale, but particularly in the USA, medical care concentrated on breeding a human stock that was fit only for domesticated life within an increasingly more costly, man-made, scientifically controlled environment. One of the main speakers at the 1970 AMA convention exhorted her pediatric colleagues to consider each newborn baby as a *patient* until the child could be certified as healthy. Hospital-born, formula-fed, antibiotic-stuffed children thus grow into adults who can breathe the air, eat the food, and survive the lifelessness of a modern city, who will breed and raise at almost any cost a generation even more dependent on medicine.

Bureaucratic medicine spread over the entire world. In 1968, after twenty years of Mao's regime, the Medical College of Shanghai had to conclude that it was engaged in the training of "so-called first-rate doctors . . . who ignore five million peasants and serve only minorities in cities. . . . They create large expenses for routine laboratory examinations . . . prescribe huge amounts of anti-

biotics unnecessarily . . . and in the absence of hospital
or laboratory facilities have to limit themselves to explain-
ing the mechanisms of the disease to people for whom they
cannot do anything, and to whom this explanation is irrelevant." In China this recognition led to a major institutional inversion. Today, the same college reports that one
million health workers have reached acceptable levels of
competence. These health workers are laymen who in periods of low agricultural manpower needs have attended
short courses, starting with the dissection of pigs, gone on
to the performance of routine lab tests, the study of the
elements of bacteriology, pathology, clinical medicine,
hygiene, and acupuncture, and continued in apprenticeship with doctors or previously trained colleagues. These
"barefoot doctors" remain at their work places but are
excused occasionally when fellow workers require their assistance. They have responsibility for environmental sanitation, for health education, immunization, first aid, primary medical care, post-illness follow-up, as well as for gyne-
cological assistance, birth control, and abortion education.
Ten years after the second watershed of Western medicine
had been acknowledged, China intends to have one fully
competent health worker for every hundred people. China
has proved that a sudden inversion of a major institution is possible. It remains to be seen if this deprofessionalization can be sustained against the overweening ideology
of unlimited progress and pressures from classical doctors
to incorporate their barefoot homonym as part-time professionals on the bottom rung of a medical hierarchy.

In the West during the sixties dissatisfaction with medicine grew in proportion to its cost, reaching the greatest
intensity in the USA. Rich foreigners flocked to the medical
centers of Boston, Houston, and Denver to seek exotic repair jobs, while the infant mortality of the U.S. poor remained comparable to that in some tropical countries of
Africa and Asia. Only the very rich in the United States
can now afford what all people in poor countries have:

personal attention around the deathbed. An American can now spend in two days of private nursing the median yearly cash income of the world's population.

Instead of exposing the systemic disorder, however, only the symptoms of "sick" medicine are now publicly indicated in the United States. Spokesmen for the poor object to the capitalist prejudices of the AMA and the income of doctors. Community leaders object to the lack of community control over the delivery systems of professional health maintenance or of sick care, believing that laymen on hospital boards can harness professional medics. Black spokesmen object to the concentration of research grants on the types of disease which tend to strike the white, elderly, overfed foundation official who approves them. They ask for research on sickle-cell anemia, which strikes only the black. The general voter hopes that the end of the war in Vietnam will make more funds available for an increase of medical production. This general concern with symptoms, however, distracts attention from the malignant expansion of *institutional* health care which is at the root of the rising costs and demands and the decline in well-being.

The crisis of medicine lies on a much deeper level than its symptoms reveal and is consistent with the present crisis of all industrial institutions. It results from the development of a professional complex supported and exhorted by society to provide increasingly "better" health, and from the willingness of clients to serve as guinea pigs in this vain experiment. People have lost the right to declare themselves sick; society now accepts their claims to sickness only after certification by medical bureaucrats.

It is not strictly necessary to this argument to accept 1913 and 1955 as the two watershed years in order to understand that early in the century medical practice emerged into an era of scientific verification of its results. And later medical science itself became an alibi for the obvious damage caused by the medical professional. At the first watershed the desirable effects of new scientific discoveries were easily measured and verified. Germ-free water reduced infant mortality related to diarrhea, aspirin reduced the pain of rheumatism, and malaria could be controlled by quinine. Some traditional cures were recognized as quackery, but, more importantly, the use of some simple habits and tools spread widely. People began to understand the relationship between health and a balanced diet, fresh air, calisthenics, pure water and soap. New devices ranging from tooth-brushes to Band-Aids and condoms became widely available. The positive contribution of modern medicine to individual health during the early part of the twentieth century can hardly be questioned.

But then medicine began to approach the second watershed. Every year medical science reported a new breakthrough. Practitioners of new specialties rehabilitated some individuals suffering from rare diseases. The practice of medicine became centered on the performance of hospital-based staffs. Trust in miracle cures obliterated good sense and traditional wisdom on healing and health care. The irresponsible use of drugs spread from doctors to the general public. The second watershed was approached when the marginal utility of further professionalization declined, at least insofar as it can be expressed in terms of the physical well-being of the largest number of people. The second watershed was superseded when the marginal *dis*utility increased as further monopoly by the medical establishment became an indicator of more suffering for larger numbers of people. After the passage of this second watershed, medicine still claimed continued progress, as measured by the new landmarks doctors set for themselves and then reached: both predictable discoveries and costs. For instance, a few patients survived longer with transplants of various organs. On the other hand, the total social cost exacted by medicine ceased to be measurable in conventional terms. Society can have no quantitative standards by which to add up the negative value of illusion, social control, prolonged suffering, loneliness, genetic deterioration, and frustration produced by medical treatment.

Other industrial institutions have passed through the

same two watersheds. This is certainly true for the major social agencies that have been reorganized according to scientific criteria during the last 150 years. Education, the mails, social work, transportation, and even civil engineering have followed this evolution. At first, new knowledge is applied to the solution of a clearly stated problem and scientific measuring sticks are applied to account for the new efficiency. But at a second point, the progress demonstrated in a previous achievement is used as a rationale for the exploitation of society as a whole in the service of a value which is determined and constantly revised by an element of society, by one of its self-certifying professional elites.

In the case of transportation it has taken almost a century to pass from an era served by motorized vehicles to the era in which society has been reduced to virtual enslavement to the car. During the American Civil War steam power on wheels became effective. The new economy in transportation enabled many people to travel by rail at the speed of a royal coach, and to do so with a comfort kings had not dared dream of. Gradually, desirable locomotion was associated and finally identified with high vehicular speeds. But when transportation had passed through its second watershed, vehicles had created more distances than they helped to bridge; more time was used by the entire society for the sake of traffic than was "saved."

It is sufficient to recognize the existence of these two watersheds in order to gain a fresh perspective on our present social crisis. In one decade several major institutions have moved jointly over their second watershed. Schools are losing their claim to be effective tools to provide education; cars have ceased to be effective tools for mass transportation; the assembly line has ceased to be an acceptable mode of production.

The characteristic reaction of the sixties to the growing frustration was further technological and bureaucratic escalation. Self-defeating escalation of power became the core-ritual practiced in highly industrialized nations. In this context the Vietnam war is both revealing and concealing. It makes this ritual visible for the entire world in a narrow theater of war, yet it also distracts attention from the same ritual being played out in many so-called peaceful arenas. The conduct of the war proves that a convivial army limited to bicycle speeds is served by the opponent's escalation of anonymous power. And yet many Americans argue that the resources squandered on the war in the Far East could be used effectively to overwhelm poverty at home. Others are anxious to use the $20 billion the war now costs for increasing international development assistance from its present low of $2 billion. They fail to grasp the underlying institutional structure common to a peaceful war on poverty and a bloody war on dissidence. Both escalate what they are meant to eliminate.

While evidence shows that more of the same leads to utter defeat, nothing less than more and more seems worthwhile in a society infected by the growth mania. The desperate plea is not only for more bombs and more police, more medical examinations and more teachers, but also for more information and research. The editor-in-chief of the *Bulletin of Atomic Scientists* claims that most of our present problems are the result of recently acquired knowledge badly applied, and concludes that the only remedy for the mess created by this information is more of it. It has become fashionable to say that where science and technology have created problems, it is only more scientific understanding and better technology that can carry us past them. The cure for bad management is more management. The cure for specialized research is more costly interdisciplinary research, just as the cure for polluted rivers is more costly nonpolluting detergents. The pooling of stores of information, the building up of a knowledge stock, the attempt to overwhelm present problems by the production of more science is the ultimate attempt to solve a crisis by escalation.

II

Convivial Reconstruction

The symptoms of accelerated crisis are widely recognized. Multiple attempts have been made to explain them. I believe that this crisis is rooted in a major twofold experiment which has failed, and I claim that the resolution of the crisis begins with a recognition of the failure. For a hundred years we have tried to make machines work for men and to school men for life in their service. Now it turns out that machines do not "work" and that people cannot be schooled for a life at the service of machines. The hypothesis on which the experiment was built must now be discarded. The hypothesis was that machines can replace slaves. The evidence shows that, used for this purpose, machines enslave men. Neither a dictatorial proletariat nor a leisure mass can escape the dominion of constantly expanding industrial tools.

The crisis can be solved only if we learn to invert the present deep structure of tools; if we give people tools that guarantee their right to work with high, independent efficiency, thus simultaneously eliminating the need for either slaves or masters and enhancing each person's range of freedom. People need new tools to work with rather than tools that "work" for them. They need technology to make the most of the energy and imagination each has, rather than more well-programmed energy slaves.

I believe that society must be reconstructed to enlarge the contribution of autonomous individuals and primary groups to the total effectiveness of a new system of production designed to satisfy the human needs which it also determines. In fact, the institutions of industrial society do just the opposite. As the power of machines increases, the role of persons more and more decreases to that of mere consumers.

Individuals need tools to move and to dwell. They need remedies for their diseases and means to communicate with one another. People cannot make all these things for themselves. They depend on being supplied with objects and services which vary from culture to culture. Some people depend on the supply of food and others on the supply of ball bearings.

People need not only to obtain things, they need above all the freedom to make things among which they can live, to give shape to them according to their own tastes, and to put them to use in caring for and about others. Prisoners in rich countries often have access to more things and services than members of their families, but they have no say in how things are to be made and cannot decide what to do with them. Their punishment consists in being deprived of what I shall call "conviviality." They are degraded to the status of mere consumers.

I choose the term "conviviality" to designate the opposite of industrial productivity. I intended it to mean autonomous and creative intercourse among persons, and the intercourse of persons with their environment; and this in contrast with the conditioned response of persons to the demands made upon them by others, and by a man-made environment. I consider conviviality to be individual freedom realized in personal interdependence and, as such, an intrinsic ethical value. I believe that, in any society, as conviviality is reduced below a certain level, no amount of industrial productivity can effectively satisfy the needs it creates among society's members.

Present institutional purposes, which hallow industrial productivity at the expense of convivial effectiveness, are a major factor in the amorphousness and meaninglessness that plague contemporary society. The increasing demand for products has come to define society's process. I will suggest how this present trend can be reversed and how modern science and technology can be used to endow human activity with unprecedented effectiveness. This reversal would permit the evolution of a life style and of a political system which give priority to the protection, the maximum use, and the enjoyment of the one resource that is almost equally distributed among all people: personal energy under personal control. I will argue that we can no longer live and work effectively without public controls over tools and institutions that curtail or negate any person's right to the creative use of his or her energy. For this purpose we need procedures to ensure that controls over the tools of society are established and governed by political process rather than by decisions by experts.

The transition to socialism cannot be effected without an inversion of our present institutions and the substitution of convivial for industrial tools. At the same time, the retooling of society will remain a pious dream unless the ideals of socialist justice prevail. I believe that the present crisis of our major institutions ought to be welcomed as a crisis of revolutionary liberation because our present institutions abridge basic human freedom for the sake of providing people with more institutional outputs. This worldwide crisis of world-wide institutions can lead to a new consciousness about the nature of tools and to majority action for their control. If tools are not controlled politically, they will be managed in a belated technocratic response to disaster. Freedom and dignity will continue to dissolve into an unprecedented enslavement of man to his tools.

As an alternative to technocratic disaster, I propose the vision of a convivial society. A convivial society would be the result of social arrangements that guarantee for each member the most ample and free access to the tools of the community and limit this freedom only in favor of another member's equal freedom.

At present people tend to relinquish the task of envisaging the future to a professional elite. They transfer power to politicians who promise to build up the machinery to deliver this future. They accept a growing range of power levels in society when inequality is needed to maintain high outputs. Political institutions themselves become draft mechanisms to press people into complicity with output goals. What is right comes to be subordinated to what is good for institutions. Justice is debased to mean the equal distribution of institutional wares.

The individual's autonomy is intolerably reduced by a society that defines the maximum satisfaction of the maximum number as the largest consumption of industrial goods. Alternate political arrangements would have the purpose of permitting all people to define the images of their own future. New politics would aim principally to exclude the design of artifacts and rules that are obstacles to the exercise of this personal freedom. Such politics would limit the scope of tools as demanded by the protection of three values: survival, justice, and self-defined work. I take these values to be fundamental to any convivial society, however different one such society might be from another in practice, institutions, or rationale.

Each of these three values imposes its own limits on tools. The *conditions for survival* are necessary but not sufficient to ensure justice; people can survive in prison. The *conditions for the just distribution* of industrial outputs are necessary, but not sufficient to promote convivial production. People can be equally enslaved by their tools. The *conditions for convivial work* are structural arrangements that make possible the just distribution of unprecedented power. A postindustrial society must and can be so constructed that no one person's ability to express him- or herself in work will require as a condition the enforced labor or the enforced learning or the enforced consumption of another.

In an age of scientific technology, the convivial structure of tools is a necessity for survival in full justice which is both distributive and participatory. This is so because science has opened new energy sources. Competition for inputs must lead to destruction, while their central control in the hands of a Leviathan would sacrifice equal control over inputs to the semblance of an equal distribution of outputs. Rationally designed convivial tools have become the basis for participatory justice.

But this does not mean that the transition from our present to a convivial mode of production can be accomplished without serious threats to the survival of many people. At present the relationship between people and their tools is suicidally distorted. The survival of Pakistanis depends on Canadian grain, and the survival of New Yorkers on world-wide exploitation of natural resources. The birth pangs of a convivial world society will inevitably be violently painful for hungry Indians and for helpless New Yorkers. I will later argue that the transition from the present mode of production, which is overwhelmingly industrial, toward conviviality may start suddenly. But for the sake of the survival of many people it will be desirable that the transition does not happen all at once. I argue that survival in justice is possible only at the cost of those sacrifices implicit in the adoption of a convivial mode of production and the universal renunciation of unlimited progeny, affluence, and power on the part of both individuals and groups. This price cannot be extorted by some despotic Leviathan, nor elicited by social engineering. People will rediscover the value of joyful sobriety and liberating austerity only if they relearn to depend on each other rather than on energy slaves. The price for a convivial society will be paid only as the result of a political process which reflects and promotes the society-wide inversion of present industrial consciousness. This political process will find its concrete expression not in some taboo, but in a series of temporary agreements on one or the other concrete limitation of means, constantly adjusted under the pressure of conflicting insights and interests.

In this volume I want to offer a methodology by which to recognize means which have turned into ends. My subject is tools and not intentions. The choice of this subject makes it impossible to undertake several related, relevant, and tempting tasks because:

1. It would not serve my purpose to describe in detail any fictional community of the future. I want to provide guidelines for action, not for fantasy. A modern society, bounded for convivial living, could generate a new flowering of surprises far beyond anyone's imagination and hope. I am not proposing a utopia, but a procedure that provides each community with the choice of its unique social arrangements.

2. I do not want to contribute to an engineering manual for the design of convivial institutions or tools, nor do I want to engage in a sales campaign for what would be obviously a better technology. My purpose is to lay down criteria by which the manipulation of people for the sake of their tools can be immediately recognized, and thus to exclude those artifacts and institutions which inevitably extinguish a convivial life style. Paradoxically, a society of simple tools that allows men to achieve purposes with energy fully under their own control is now difficult to imagine. Our imaginations have been industrially deformed to conceive only what can be molded into an engineered system of social habits that fit the logic of large-scale production. We have almost lost the ability to frame in fancy a world in which sound and shared reasoning sets limits to everybody's power to interfere with anybody's equal power to shape the world.

The present world is divided into those who do not have enough and those who have more than enough, those who are pushed off the road by cars and those who drive them. The have-nots are miserable and the rich anxious to get more. A society whose members know what is enough might be poor, but its members would be equally free. Men with industrially distorted minds cannot grasp the rich texture of personal accomplishments within the range of modern though limited tools. There is no room in their imaginations for the qualitative change that the acceptance of a stable-state industry would mean; a society in which members are free from most of the multiple restraints of schedules and therapies now imposed for the sake of growing tools. Much less do most of our contemporaries experience the sober joy of life in this voluntary though relative poverty which lies within our grasp.

3. I will focus on the structure of tools, not on the character structure of their users. The use of industrial tools stamps in an identical way the landscape of cities each having its own history and culture. Highways, hospital wards, classrooms, office buildings, apartments, and stores look everywhere the same. Identical tools also promote the development of the same character types. Policemen in patrol cars or accountants at computers look and act alike all over the world, while their poor cousins using nightstick or pen are different from region to region. The progressive homogenization of personalities and personal relationships cannot be stemmed without a retooling of society. Research on the social character traits that make retooling difficult or doubtful is complementary to what I propose. But I am not postulating the creation of a new man as a condition for a new society, nor am I pretending to know how either social character or cultures will change. A pluralism of limited tools and of convivial commonweals would of necessity encourage a diversity of life styles.

4. It would distract from the core of my argument if I were to deal with political strategies or tactics. With the possible exception of China under Mao, no present government could restructure society along convivial lines. The managers of our major tools—nations, corporations, parties, structured movements, professions—hold power. This power is vested in the maintenance of the growth-oriented structures which they manipulate. These managers have the power to make major decisions; they can

generate new demands for the output of their tools and enforce the creation of new social labels to fit them. They can even go so far as to limit the output of tools in the interest of maximizing benefits. But they have no power to reverse the basic structure of the institutional arrangements which they manage.

The major institutions now optimize the output of large tools for lifeless people. Their inversion implies institutions that would foster the use of individually accessible tools to support the meaningful and responsible deeds of fully awake people. Turning basic institutions upside down and inside out is what the adoption of a convivial mode of production would require. Such an inversion of society is beyond the managers of present institutions.

Today's managers form a new class of men, selected for their character, competence, and interest—which enable them to both expand the productive society and promote the further operant conditioning of their clients. They hold and manage power no matter who lives in the illusion that he owns the tools. This class of power-holders must be eliminated, but this cannot be done by mass slaughter or replacement. The new elite would only claim more legitimacy in the manipulation of the inherited structured power. Management can be done away with only by eliminating the machinery that makes it necessary and, therefore, the demands for output that give it sway. In a convivial society there is little need for replacing the chairman of the board.

In a society in which power—both political and physical—is bounded and spread by political decision there is place not only for a new flowering of products and characters, but also for a variety in forms of governance. Certainly, new tools would provide new options. Convivial tools rule out certain levels of power, compulsion, and programming, which are precisely those features that now tend to make all governments look more or less alike. But the adoption of a convivial mode of production does not of itself mean that one specific form of government would be more fitting than another, nor does it rule out a world federation, or agreements between nation-states, or communes, or many of the most traditional forms of governance. I restrict myself to the description of basic structural criteria within which the retooling of society can be achieved.

5. A methodology by which to recognize when corporate tools become destructive of society itself requires the recognition of the value of distributory and participatory justice. I believe that my succinct statement will be sufficient to identify necessary restraints on tools, but it will also preclude that in this essay I reach any conclusion about a desirable degree of subordination of means to ends.

6. The economics applicable to a postindustrial and convivial society can neither be ignored nor taken for granted. In a society that accepts politically defined limits on all types of industrial growth, many accepted terms will have to be redefined, but it is certain that in such a society inequality will not be excluded. In fact, each individual's power to make effective changes would be greater than in preindustrial or in industrial times. Though they would be bounded, common tools would be incomparably more efficient than primitive, and more widely distributed than industrial, devices. Their products would accrue more to some than to others. The task of keeping net transfer of power within bounds requires the use of traditional as well as new economic devices. It will be argued that the limitation of tools cannot be effected before a corresponding new economic theory has been elaborated and has become operational. This is correct. I do propose that we use a dimensional analysis to obtain information about the major variables which can upset the balance of life, and that we rely on political process to identify the significant dimensions which man can control. I therefore propose an approach to the relationship between man's ends and his means

in which the key units of economics come to signify a dimensionless set of factors. Economics useful for the inversion of our present institutional structure starts out from politically defined limiting criteria. It is on these negative design criteria for technological devices that I want to focus attention.

A methodology, by which to recognize the public perversion of tools into purposes, encounters resistance on the part of people who are used to measuring what is good in terms of dollars. Plato knew that the bad statesman is he who believes that the art of measurement is universal, and who jumbles together what is greater or smaller and what is more fit to the purpose. Our present attitudes toward production have been formed over the centuries. Increasingly, institutions have not only shaped our demands but also in the most literal sense our logic, or sense of proportion. Having come to demand what institutions can produce, we soon believe that we cannot do without it.

The invention of education is an example of what I mean. We often forget that education acquired its present sense only recently. It was unknown before the Reformation, except as that part of early upbringing which is common to piglets, ducks, and men. It was clearly distinguished from the instruction needed by the young, and from the study in which some engaged later on in life and for which a teacher was needed. Voltaire still called it a presumptuous neologism, used only by pretentious schoolmasters.

The endeavor to put all men through successive stages of enlightenment is rooted deeply in alchemy, the Great Art of the waning Middle Ages. John Amos Comenius, a Moravian bishop of the seventeenth century, a self-styled pansophist and pedagogue, is rightly considered one of the founders of the modern school. He was among the first to propose seven or twelve grades of compulsory learning. In his *Magna Didactica* he described schools as devices to "teach everybody everything" and outlined a blueprint for the assembly-line production of knowledge, which according to his method would make education cheaper and better and make growth into full humanity possible for all. But Comenius was not only an early theoretician of mass production, he was an alchemist who adapted the technical language of his craft to describe the art of rearing children. The alchemist sought to refine base elements by graduating their spirits through twelve stages of successive enlightenment, so that for their own and all the world's benefit they might be transformed into gold. Of course, alchemists failed no matter how often they tried, but each time their "science" yielded new reasons for their failure, and they tried again.

The industrial mode of production was first fully rationalized in the manufacture of a new invisible commodity, called "education." Pedagogy opened a new chapter in the history of the *Ars Magna*. Education became the search for an alchemic process that would bring forth a new type of man who would fit into an environment created by scientific magic. But no matter how much each generation spent on its schools, it always turned out that the majority of people were certified as unfit for higher grades of enlightenment and had to be discarded as unprepared for the good life in a man-made world.

Not only has the redefinition of learning as schooling made schools seem necessary, it has also compounded the poverty of the unschooled with discrimination against the uneducated. People who have climbed up the ladder of schooling know where they dropped out and how uneducated they are. Once they accept the authority of an agency to define and measure their level of knowledge, they easily go on to accept the authority of other agencies to define for them their level of appropriate health or mobility. It is difficult for them to identify the structural corruption of our major institutions. Just as they come to believe in the value of the "knowledge stock" they acquired in school, so they come to believe that higher speeds save time and that income levels define well-being or, as an alternative, that the production of more services rather than more goods increases the quality of life.

The commodity called "education" and the institution called "school" make each other necessary. The circle can be broken only by a widely shared insight that the institution has come to define the purpose. Values abstractly stated are reduced to mechanical processes that enslave men. This serfdom can be broken only by the joyful self-recognition of the fool who assumes personal responsibility for his folly.

The institutional definition of values has made it difficult to focus our attention on the deep structure of social means. It is hard to imagine that the division of sciences, of labor, and of professions has gone too far. It is difficult to conceive of higher social effectiveness with lower industrial efficiency. To recognize the nature of desirable limits to specialization and output, we must focus our attention on the industrially determined shape of our expectations. Only then can we recognize that the emergence of a convivial and pluralist mode of production will follow the limitation of industrial institutions.

In the past, convivial life for some inevitably demanded the servitude of others. Labor efficiency was low before the steel ax, the pump, the bicycle, and the nylon fishing line. Between the High Middle Ages and the Enlightenment, the alchemic dream misled many otherwise authentic Western humanists. The illusion prevailed that the machine was a laboratory-made homunculus, and that it could do our labor instead of slaves. It is now time to correct this mistake and shake off the illusion that men are born to be slaveholders and that the only thing wrong in the past was that not all men could be equally so. By reducing our expectations of machines, however, we must guard against falling into the equally damaging rejection of all machines as if they were works of the devil.

A convivial society should be designed to allow all its members the most autonomous action by means of tools least controlled by others. People feel joy, as opposed to mere pleasure, to the extent that their activities are creative; while the growth of tools beyond a certain point increases regimentation, dependence, exploitation, and impotence. I use the term "tool" broadly enough to include not only simple hardware such as drills, pots, syringes, brooms, building elements, or motors, and not just large machines like cars or power stations; I also include among tools productive institutions such as factories that produce tangible commodities like corn flakes or electric current, and productive systems for intangible commodities such as those which produce "education," "health," "knowledge," or "decisions." I use this term because it allows me to subsume into one category all rationally designed devices, be they artifacts or rules, codes or operators, and to distinguish all these planned and engineered instrumentalities from other things such as basic food or implements, which in a given culture are not deemed to be subject to rationalization. School curricula or marriage laws are no less purposely shaped social devices than road networks.

Tools are intrinsic to social relationships. An individual relates himself in action to his society through the use of tools that he actively masters, or by which he is passively acted upon. To the degree that he masters his tools, he can invest the world with his meaning; to the degree that he is mastered by his tools, the shape of the tool determines his own self-image. Convivial tools are those which give each person who uses them the greatest opportunity to enrich the environment with the fruits of his or her vision. Industrial tools deny this possibility to those who use them and they allow their designers to determine the meaning and expectations of others. Most tools today cannot be used in a convivial fashion.

Hand tools are those which adapt man's metabolic energy to a specific task. They can be multipurpose, like some primitive hammers or good modern pocket knives, or again they can be highly specific in design such as spindles, looms, or pedal-driven sewing machines, and dentists' drills. They can also be complex such as a transportation system built to get the most in mobility out of human energy—for instance, a bicycle system composed of a series of man-powered vehicles, such as pushcarts and three-wheel rickshas, with a corresponding road system equipped with repair stations and perhaps even covered roadways. Hand tools are mere transducers of the energy generated by man's extremities and fed by the intake of air and of nourishment.

Power tools are moved, at least partially, by energy converted outside the human body. Some of them act as amplifiers of human energy: the oxen pull the plow, but man works with the oxen—the result is obtained by pooling the powers of beast and man. Power saws and motor pulleys are used in the same fashion. On the other hand, the energy used to steer a jet plane has ceased to be a significant fraction of its power output. The pilot is reduced to a mere operator guided by data which a computer digests for him. The machine needs him for lack of a better computer; or he is in the cockpit because the social control of unions over airplanes imposes his presence.

Tools foster conviviality to the extent to which they can be easily used, by anybody, as often or as seldom as desired, for the accomplishment of a purpose chosen by the user. The use of such tools by one person does not restrain another from using them equally. They do not require previous certification of the user. Their existence does not impose any obligation to use them. They allow the user to express his meaning in action.

Some institutions are structurally convivial tools. The telephone is an example. Anybody can dial the person of his choice if he can afford a coin. If untiring computers keep the lines occupied and thereby restrict the number of personal conversations, this is a misuse by the company of a license given so that persons can speak. The telephone lets anybody say what he wants to the person of his choice; he can conduct business, express love, or pick a quarrel. It is impossible for bureaucrats to define what people say to each other on the phone, even though they can interfere with—or protect—the privacy of their exchange.

Most hand tools lend themselves to convivial use unless they are artificially restricted through some institutional arrangements. They can be restricted by becoming the monopoly of one profession, as happens with dentist drills through the requirement of a license and with libraries or laboratories by placing them within schools. Also, tools can be purposely limited when simple pliers and screwdrivers are insufficient to repair modern cars. This institutional monopoly or manipulation usually constitutes an abuse and changes the nature of the tool as little as the nature of the knife is changed by its abuse for murder.

In principle the distinction between convivial and manipulatory tools is independent of the level of technology of the tool. What has been said of the telephone could be repeated point by point for the mails or for a typical Mexican market. Each is an institutional arrangement that maximizes liberty, even though in a broader context it can be abused for purposes of manipulation and control. The telephone is the result of advanced engineering; the mails require in principle little technology and considerable organization and scheduling; the Mexican market runs with minimum planning along customary patterns.

Any institution that moves toward its second watershed tends to become highly manipulative. For instance, it costs more to make teaching possible than to teach. The cost of roles exceeds the cost of production. Increasingly, components intended for the accomplishment of institutional purposes are redesigned so that they cannot be used independently. People without cars have no access to planes, and people without plane tickets have no access to convention hotels. Alternate tools which are fit to accomplish the same purposes with fewer claims are pushed off the market. For instance, civilized correspondence becomes a lost art. During the last several years this barring of alternatives has usually coincided with the increased power of the tool and the development of more complex tool systems.

It is possible that not every means of desirable production in a postindustrial society would fit the criteria of conviviality. It is probable that even in an overwhelmingly convivial world some communities would choose greater affluence at the cost of some restrictions on creativity. It is almost certain that in a period of transition from the present to the future mode of production in certain countries electricity would not commonly be produced in the backyard. It is also true that trains must run on tracks and stop on schedule at a limited number of points. Oceangoing vessels are built for one purpose; if they were sailing clippers, they might be even more specialized for one route than are present tankers. Telephone systems are highly determined for the transmission of messages of a certain band width and must be centrally administered even if they are limited to the service of only one area. It is a mistake to believe that all large tools and all centralized production would have to be excluded from a convivial society. It would equally be a mistake to demand that for the sake of conviviality the distribution of industrial goods and services be reduced to the minimum consistent with survival in order to protect the maximum equal right to self-determined participation. Different balances between distributive justice and participatory justice can prevail in societies equally striving for postindustrial conviviality, depending on the history, political ideals, and physical resources of a community.

What is fundamental to a convivial society is not the total absence of manipulative institutions and addictive goods and services, but the balance between those tools which create the specific demands they are specialized to satisfy and those complementary, enabling tools which foster self-realization. The first set of tools produces according to abstract plans for men in general; the other set enhances the ability of people to pursue their own goals in their unique way.

The criteria by which anticonvivial or manipulative tools are recognized cannot be used to exclude every tool that meets them. These criteria, however, can be applied as guidelines for structuring the totality of tools by which a society desires to define the style and level of its conviviality.

A convivial society does not exclude all schools. It does exclude a school system which has been perverted into a compulsory tool, denying privileges to the dropout. A convivial society does not exclude some high-speed intercity transport, as long as its layout does not in fact impose equally high speeds on all other routes. Not even television must be ruled out—although it permits very few programmers and speakers to define what their viewers may see—as long as the over-all structure of society does not favor the degradation of everyone into a compulsory voyeur. The criteria of conviviality are to be considered as guidelines to the continuous process by which a society's members defend their liberty, and not as a set of prescriptions which can be mechanically applied.

At present the reverse guideline prevails, even in societies where the producer is told that he is in the saddle. The socialist planner competes with the free-market advocate in claiming that a society run on his principles is more productive. In 1931 Stalin translated "control over the means of production" to mean the increase of productivity by new methods used to control the producer. In the midst of the U.S. Depression he launched Russia on an industrial race. Since then a socialist policy has been considered one which serves the industrially organized productivity of a socialist country. Stalin's reinterpretation of Marxism has since then served as a form of blackmail against socialists and the left. It remains to be seen if after Mao's death China will also trade productive conviviality for institutional productivity. The Stalinist interpretation of socialism has made it possible for socialists and capitalists alike to agree on how to measure the level of development a society has achieved. Societies in which most people depend for most of their goods and services on the personal whim, kindness, or skill of another are called "underdeveloped," while those in which living has been transformed into a process of ordering from an all-encompassing store catalogue are called "advanced." Stalinism makes it possible to interpret as revolutionary whatever increases the amount of schooling, expands the road systems, or increases the productivity of extraction and manufacture. To be revolutionary has come to mean either to champion the nation that lags in production and to make its members keenly aware of the lag, or to inflame the frantic and frustrated attempts of underconsuming minorities in rich countries to catch up.

Every aspect of industrial societies has become part of a larval system for escalating production and increasing the demand necessary to justify the total social cost. For this reason, criticism of bad management, official dishonesty, insufficient research, or technological lag distracts public attention from the one issue that counts: careful analysis of the basic structure of tools as means. It is equally distracting to suggest that the present frustration is primarily due to the private ownership of the means of production, and that the public ownership of these same factories under the tutelage of a planning board could protect the interest of the majority and lead society to an equally shared abundance. As long as Ford Motor Company can be condemned simply because it makes Ford rich, the illusion is bolstered that the same factory could make the public rich. As long as people believe that the public can profit from cars, they will not condemn Ford for making cars. The issue at hand is not the juridical ownership of tools, but rather the discovery of the characteristic of some tools which make it impossible for anybody to "own" them. The concept of ownership cannot be applied to a tool that cannot be controlled. The issue at hand, therefore, is what tools can be controlled in the public interest. Only secondarily does the question arise whether private control of a potentially useful tool is in the public interest.

Certain tools are destructive no matter who owns them, whether it be the Mafia, stockholders, a foreign company, the state, or even a workers' commune. Networks of multi-lane highways, long-range, wide-band-width transmitters, strip mines, or compulsory school systems are such tools. Destructive tools must inevitably increase regimentation, dependence, exploitation, or impotence, and rob not only the rich but also the poor of conviviality, which is the primary treasure in many so-called underdeveloped areas.

It has become difficult for contemporary man to imagine development and modernization in terms of lower rather than higher energy use. High technology has been mistakenly identified with powerful intervention in physical, psychological, and social processes. The illusion that a high culture is one that uses the highest possible quantities of energy must be overcome if we are to get tools into focus. In classical societies power sources were very equally distributed. Each man was born with the potential to use most of the power he would need in a lifetime if his organism was properly maintained. Control over larger amounts of physical energy was the result of psychic manipulation or of political domination.

Men did not need power tools to build the Mexican pyramids of Teotihuacán or the Philippine rice terraces of Ibagué. Their muscles provided the force to raise St. Peter's and to dig the channels of Angkor Vat. Runners carried the messages between Caesar's generals and between village chiefs and Inca planners. Hands and feet moved the spindle and the loom, the pottery wheel and the saw. Human metabolism provided the energy that powered classical agriculture, manufacture, and war. Individual skills were the controls that shaped animal energy into socially defined work. The energy that rulers could control was the sum of the performance their subjects voluntarily or involuntarily conceded.

I do not claim that human metabolism provided all useful power, but I do claim that in most cultures it was the main source of power. Men knew how to harness some of the forces of the environment. They steered barges down the Nile; they gentled beasts to draw the plow; they caught the wind in their sails; they became experts in the construction of simple machines which combined the power of men and of rain and of gravity. They also tamed fire in the forge and the kitchen, but the total output of these sources remained secondary. Even Mongols who lived on their mounts provided more energy with their muscles than with their horsepower. All the energy tapped from the environment to build Athens and Florence did not contribute as much controlled power to these classical societies as did their men. Only when man lit fires to turn cities into ruins or jungles into swiddens did he release—but certainly not control—energies that overwhelmed the power of the people who used them.

The amount of physical power available to old societies can be estimated. It can be expressed in multiples of the average man's working time and metabolic energy. He can burn 2,500 calories a day, four-fifths of them just to stay alive. They go into making his heart beat and his brain pulse. The remainder can be externalized, but this does not mean that all of it can be transformed into work. A large portion of the lifetime capacity of a man to act on his physical and social environment is burnt running around while he grows up. More is spent for chores that lie beyond his personal choice—but also beyond other men's reach. He consumes energy in getting up, in preparing food, in seeking protection from the cold, or in avoiding the slavedriver's whip. If man is deprived of the use of this power, he becomes useless for work. Society can give shape to these personal activities, but it cannot appropriate the energy used on them for other tasks. Custom, language, and law can determine the form of the slave's pottery, but the master cannot take the last pots or the roof away from his slaves, not if he wants them to go on slaving for him. A small energy parcel from each man was the major source of physical power with which temples were built, mountains were moved, cloth was woven, wars were waged, and kings were carried around or amused.

Power was limited. It was proportional to the population. Its major source was the muscles of individual men. Its efficient use depended on the stage of development which hand tools had reached and the distribution of necessary tools throughout the population. Tools all matched the impedance of manpower to the task. Except by redirecting the forces of gravity and wind they did not and could not act as amplifiers of this power. To control more power than others in his society, a man had to lord it over his fellows. If a ruler could draw power from sources other than men, his control over this power still depended on his control over men. Each pair of oxen required a man to lead them. Even the forge needed a boy to blow into the fire. Political control coincided with the control over physical power, and the control of power depended entirely on authority.

Equal power and equal direct control of power were both features of preindustrial societies, but this did not guarantee an equal autonomy in the exercise of this control. On a very primitive level the physical predominance of one person made him into the lord of others. A slight advantage in organization or weaponry made one people the master of another. The appropriation of resources and tools created the basis of class societies and fostered the rituals and myths that shaped men to fit into the class to which they were assigned.

In a preindustrial society political control could extend only over the excess power that people could produce. As soon as a population became efficient enough to produce more power than was required to maintain it, people could be deprived of control over this energy. They could be compelled to cede their power to the decisions of others. They could be either taxed or enslaved. Part of what they produced on their own could be taken from them, or they could be put to work for the king or the village. Ideology, economic structure, and life style tended to favor this concentration of excess energy under the control of a few.

The degree to which this concentration of control polarized social benefits varied from one culture to another. At best it improved the range within which most members of society could employ their remaining energies. High peasant cultures offer good examples. While all shared in the tasks of defending their land from enemies or floods, each was also better dressed, housed, and fed. At worst, the concentration of decisions over power led to the establishment of empires which were expanded by mercenaries and fed from plantations worked by slaves.

The total energy available to society increased rapidly toward the end of the Iron Age, that is, between the time of Agrippa and the time of Watt. Most of the radical technical mutations that came into existence before the scientific discoveries in the field of electricity in fact came about early in the Middle Ages. Because they used windpower far more effectively than any previous invention, three-masted sailing ships made world-wide transportation possible. Speedy transportation with regular deliveries was made possible by the building of canals in Europe, a millennium after the same discovery was implemented in Southeast Asia. A vastly increased application of nonhuman energy to industries like brewing, dyeing, pottery-making, brick-making, sugar-refining, salt manufacture, and transportation went parallel with the construction of vastly improved water wheels and windmills.

From the High Middle Ages to the late Renaissance, new social tools developed that ensured the protection of the worker's self-image and dignity, although he was now sometimes dwarfed by the size of machines. The guild system did indeed give the worker a new claim to the monopoly over tools specific to his trade. But the mill had not yet grown out of proportion to the miller. His monopoly over grain-processing protected the guildsman, provided him with extra holidays, and still maximized the services that he could render to his town. Guilds were neither unions nor professional associations.

Lewis Mumford in his *The Myth of the Machine: The Pentagon of Power* points out that one particular enterprise, namely mining,

> set the pattern for later modes of mechanization by its callous disregard for human factors, by its indifference to the pollution and destruction of the neighboring environment, by its concentration upon the physico-chemical process for obtaining the desired metal or fuel,

and above all by its topographic and mental isolation
from the organic world of the farmer and the crafts-
man, and the spiritual world of the Church, the University and the City. In its destruction of the environment and its indifference to the risks to human life,
mining closely resembles warfare—though likewise it
often, through its confrontation of danger and death,
brings into existence a tough, self-respecting personality
. . . the soldier at his best. But the destructive animus
of mining and its punishing routine of work, along
with its environmental poverty and disorder were passed
on to the new industries that used its products. These
negative social results offset the mechanical gains.

This new attitude toward gainful activity is well reflected
in the introduction of a new term to designate it. *Tripaliare*
meant to torture on the *trepalium*, which was first men-
tioned in the sixth century as an instrument of impalement
made out of three wooden sticks. By the twelfth century the
word in both French and Spanish expressed a painful experience to which man is subjected; only in the sixteenth
century did it become possible to use the verb *trabajar* inter-
changeably with *laborar* and *sudar* on the job. Equally significant is what happened in the English language. Things
began to *work*—first medicines (1600) and then physical
tools (1650), even though these were not yet tools driven by
any outside power. The alchemist's dream of making a homunculus in the test tube slowly took the shape of creating
robots to *work* for man, and to educate men to *work* along-
side them. The ideology of an industrial organization of
tools and a capitalist organization of the economy preceded
by many centuries what is usually called the Industrial Revolution. On Baconian premises Europeans began, according to Mumford, to save time, shrink space, augment power,
multiply goods, overthrow organic norms and displace real
organisms with mechanisms that stimulated them or vastly
magnified some single function they performed. All these
imperatives, which have become the groundwork of science

as technology in our present society, seem axiomatic and absolute only because they remain unexamined. The same change of mind appears also in a transfer from ritual regularity to mechanical regularity with an emphasis on time-keeping, space-measuring, account-keeping, thus translating concrete objects and complex events into abstract quantities. According to Mumford, it was this capitalistic devotion to repetitive order that helped undermine the unmeasurable personal balance between the workman and his tools.

New power meant a new relation to time. The lending of money against interest was considered "against nature" by the Church: money naturally was a means of exchange to buy necessities, not a capital that could *work* or bear fruits. During the seventeenth century even the Church abandoned this view—though reluctantly—to accept the fact that Christians had become capitalist merchants. Time became like money: I now can *have* a few hours before lunch; how shall I *spend* time? . . . I am *short of* time so I can't *afford* to *spend* that much time on a committee; it's not *worth* the time! . . . It would be a *waste* of time; I'd rather *save* an hour.

Scientists began to consider man as a power source. They sought to measure the maximum daily exertion that might be expected from a man and compare both his maintenance and his power to those of a horse. Man was reinvented as a source of mechanical power. Prisoners condemned to the galleys were not much use most of the time, since galleys were most of the time in port. Prisoners condemned to the treadmills produced rotary power to which any of the new machines could be hooked. Up to the early nineteenth century men in English prisons actually labored on the treadmills to make machines work.

The new attitude of man to his tools during the Industrial Revolution, which began as capitalism did in the fifteenth century, finally called for the invention of new sources of power. The steam engine was a product of the Industrial Revolution rather than the cause of it. Power plants soon became mobile, and with the railroad the Iron Age and the Industrial Revolution came to an end. Industrial ways became the status quo.

Immense new sources of power were tapped during the twentieth century, and much of this power became self-governing. Man has now been almost replaced by machines and reduced to being their operator. Fewer men are needed as gang workers in the fields: slavery has become uneconomical. But also fewer men are needed on the assembly line, as engineers have designed machines to perform the tasks that mass production and industrialization had created in the centuries before the steam engine. More power has become available, so more power is used. The human slaveowner is replaced by the operant conditioning of men in the megamachine.

We have all grown up as children of our time, and therefore it is extremely difficult to envisage a postindustrial yet human type of "work." To reduce industrial tools seems equivalent to a return to the tortured labor of the mine and the factory, or to the labor of the U.S. farmhand who has to compete with his mechanical neighbor. The worker who had to dip a heavy tire into a solution of hot sulfur each time the machine asked for it was literally hooked onto his apparatus. Agricultural labor also ceased to be what it was for a slave or a farmer. For the slave it was *labor* at the service and behest of a master; for the peasant it was his own *work* which he could organize and shape in accordance with the demands of growing plants, hungry animals, and unpredictable weather. The modern farmhand in the United States today who is deprived of power tools is under a double pressure quite different from that of the classical slave: he must measure up to performance standards set by farmhands elsewhere who use machines, and he is constantly aware that he is underprivileged, exploited, and abused because in an age of the megamachine he feels that he is used like a component. The prospect that moving toward a convivial society might imply a society with low power tools would seem to him like a return to the exploitation of manpower by inefficient industrial machines in the early periods of steam.

I have described three types of institutional arrangements within which tools can be used. Certain tools can be used effectively within only one of these arrangements. There are tools which can be used normally for fully satisfying, imaginative, and independent *work;* others tend to be used primarily in activities best labeled as *labor;* and, finally, certain machines can only be *operated.* The same can be said about physical artifacts and about the set of rules that define formal institutional arrangements. Cars are machines that call for highways, and highways pretend to be public utilities while in fact they are discriminatory devices. Compulsory schools constitute a huge bureaucratic system; no matter how convivially a teacher tries to conduct his class, his pupils learn through him to which class they belong. Cars *operate* on highways as teachers operate in schools. Only in a very limited sense can what the truck driver and the teacher do be called *labor.* Only exceptionally will a teacher feel that his operations within the school system do not directly interfere with his *work.*

The market characteristics of these three types of human activity help to clarify the distinction among them. Labor can be purchased or sold in the marketplace. Not work as an activity, but only the result of convivial work can be marketed. Finally, the right to operate machines and to obtain the scarce privileges that go with employment must be earned through the previous consumption of certified treatments, which take the form of a curriculum of schooling and testing along with successive jobs.

Tools for a convivial and yet efficient society could not have been designed at an earlier stage of history. We now can design the machinery for eliminating slavery without enslaving man to the machine. Science and technology are not bound to the peculiar notion, seemingly characteristic of the last 150 years of their application to production, that new knowledge of nature's laws has to be locked into increasingly more specialized and highly capitalized preparation of men to use them. The sciences, which specialized out of philosophy, have become the rationale for an increasing division of operations. The division of labor has finally led to the labor-*saving* division of tools. New technology is now used to amplify supply funnels for commodities. Public utilities are turned from facilities for persons into arenas for the owners of expensive tools. The use of science and technology constantly supports the industrial mode of production, and thereby crowds off the scene all tool shops for independent enterprise. But this is not the necessary result of new scientific discoveries or of their useful application. It is rather the result of a total prejudice in favor of the future expansion of an industrial mode of production. Research teams are organized to remedy minor inefficiencies that hold up the further growth of a specific production process. These planned discoveries are then heralded as costly breakthroughs in the interest of further public service. Research is now mostly oriented toward industrial development.

This unqualified identification of scientific advance with the replacement of human initiative by programmed tools springs from an ideological prejudice and is not the result of scientific analysis. Science could be applied for precisely the opposite purpose. Advanced or "high" technology could become identified with labor-sparing, work-intensive decentralized productivity. Natural and social science can be used for the creation of tools, utilities, and rules available to everyone, permitting individuals and transient associations to constantly recreate their mutual relationships and their environment with unenvisaged freedom and self-expression.

New understanding of nature can now be applied to our tools either for the purpose of propelling us into a hyper-industrial age of electronic cybernetics or to help us develop a wide range of truly modern and yet convivial tools. Limited resources can be used to provide millions of viewers with the color image of one performer or to provide many people with free access to the records of their choice. In the first case, technology will be used for the further promotion of the specialized worker, be he a plumber, surgeon, or TV performer. More and more bureaucrats will study the market, consult their balance sheets, and decide for more people on more occasions about the range of products among which they may choose. There will be a further increase of useful things for useless people. But science can also be used to simplify tools and to enable the layman to shape his immediate environment to his taste. The time has come to take the syringe out of the hand of the doctor, as the pen was taken out of the hand of the scribe during the Reformation in Europe.

Most curable sickness can now be diagnosed and treated by laymen. People find it so difficult to accept this statement because the complexity of medical ritual has hidden from them the simplicity of its basic procedures. It took the example of the barefoot doctor in China to show how modern practice by simple workers in their spare time could, in three years, catapult health care in China to levels unparalleled elsewhere. In most other countries health care by laymen is considered a crime. A 17-year-old friend of mine was recently tried for having treated some 130 of her high school colleagues for VD. She was acquitted on a technicality by the judge when expert counsel compared her performance with that of the U.S. Health Service. Nowhere in the USA can her achievement be considered "standard," because she succeeded in making retests on all her patients six weeks after their first treatment. Progress *should* mean growing competence in self-care rather than growing dependence.

The possibilities of lay therapy also run up against our commitment to "better" health, and have blinded us to the distinction between curable and incurable sickness. This is a crucial distinction because as soon as a doctor treats incurable sickness, he perverts his craft from a means to an end. He becomes a charlatan set on providing scientific consolation in a ceremony in which the doctor takes on the patient's struggle against death. The patient becomes the object of his ministrations instead of a sick subject who can be helped in the process of healing or dying. Medicine ceases to be a legitimate profession when it cannot provide each man or his next of kin with the tool to make this one crucial differential diagnosis for himself.

New opportunities for the progressive expansion of lay therapy and the parallel progressive reduction of professional medicine are rejected because life in an industrial society has made us place such exaggerated value on standard products, uniformity, and certified quality. Industrialized expectations have blurred the distinction between personal vocation and standard profession. Of course, any layman can grow up to become a general healer, but this does not mean that every layman must be taught how to heal. It simply means that in a society in which people can and must take care of their neighbors and do so on their own, some people will excel at using the best available tools. In a society in which people can once again be born in their homes and die in their homes and in which there is a place for cripples and idiots in the street, and where a distinction is made between plumbing and healing, quite a few people would grow up capable of assisting others to heal, to suffer, or to die.

Just as with proper social arrangements most people would grow up as readers without having to be schooled and without having to recreate the pre-Gutenberg profession of the scribe, so a sufficient number would grow up competent with medical tools. This would make healing so plentiful that it would be difficult to turn this competence into a monopoly or to sell it as a commodity. Deprofessionalization means a renewed distinction between the freedom of vocation and the occasional boost sick people derive from the quasi-religious authority of the certified doctor.

Of course the deprofessionalization of most ordinary medicine could sometimes substitute a quack for today's impostor, but the threat of quackery becomes less convincing as professionally caused damage grows. There just is no substitute for the self-correcting judgment of the layman in socializing the tools invented or used by the professional. Lifelong familiarity with the specific dangers of a specific remedy is the best preparation for accepting or rejecting it in time of crisis.

Take another tool—transportation—as an example. Under President Cárdenas in the early thirties, Mexico developed a modern system of transportation. Within a few years about 80 percent of the population had gained access to the advantages of the automobile. Most important, villages had been connected by dirt roads or tracks. Heavy, simple, and tough trucks traveled over them every now and then, moving at speeds far below twenty miles per hour. People were crowded together on rows of wooden benches nailed to the floor to make place for merchandise loaded in the back and on the roof. Over short distances the vehicle could not compete with people, who had been used to walking and to carrying their merchandise, but long-distance travel had become possible for all. Instead of a man driving his pig to market, man and pig could go together in a truck. Any Mexican could now reach any point in his country in a few days.

Since 1945 the money spent on roads has increased every year. It has been used to build highways between a few major centers. Fragile cars now move at high speeds over smooth roads. Large, specialized trucks connect factories. The old, all-purpose tramp truck has been pushed back into the mountains or swamps. In most areas either the peasant must take a bus to go to the market to buy industrially packaged commodities, or he sells his pig to the trucker in the employ of the meat merchant. He can no longer go to town with his pig. He pays taxes for the roads which serve the owners of various specialized monopolies and does so under the illusion that the benefits will ultimately spread to him.

In exchange for an occasional ride on an upholstered seat in an air-conditioned bus, the common man has lost much of the mobility the old system gave him, without gaining any new freedom. Research done in two typical large states of Mexico—one dominated by deserts, the other by mountains and lush growth—confirms this conclusion. Less than 1 percent of the population in either state traveled a distance of over 15 miles in any one hour during 1970. More appropriate pushcarts and bicycles, both motorized when needed, would have presented a technologically much more efficient solution for 99 percent of the population than the vaunted highway development. Such pushcarts could have been built and maintained by people trained on the job, and operated on roadbeds built to Inca standards, yet covered to diminish drag. The usual rationale given for the investment in standard roads and cars is that it is a condition for development and that without it a region cannot be integrated into the world market. Both claims are true, but can be considered as desirable only if monetary integration is the goal of development.

During the last few years the promoters of development have come to admit that cars, as operated now, are inefficient. This inefficiency is blamed on the fact that modern vehicles are designed for private ownership, not for the public good. In fact, modern personnel transport is inefficient not because an individual capsule rather than a cabin is the model for the largest number of vehicles, or because these vehicles are now owned by their drivers. It is inefficient because of the obsessive identification of higher speed with better transport. Just as the demand for better health at all costs is a form of mental sickness, so is the pretense of higher speed.

The railroads reflected the class societies they served simply by putting different fares on the same speed. But when a society commits itself to higher speeds, the speedometer becomes an indicator of social class. Any peasant could accompany Lázaro Cárdenas on horseback. Today only his personal staff can accompany a modern governor in his private helicopter. In capitalist countries how often you can cover great distances is determined by what you can pay. In socialist countries your velocity depends on the social importance the bureaucracy attaches to you. In both cases the particular speed at which you travel puts you into your class and company. Speed is one of the means by which an efficiency-oriented society is stratified.

Fostered addiction to speed is also a means of social control. Transportation in its various forms now swallows 23 percent of the U.S. gross expenditures. The United States may be rich enough to allocate one-fourth of its energy resources and human time to the enterprise of getting somewhere. Under Khufu, Egyptians might have spent that much during a few years to build the Great Pyramid and to get their ruler to the underworld. Unfortunately, however, transportation exacts an ever higher percentage of the cash spent in a given year within many a Latin American municipality. The road degrades the subsistence farmer and artisan, integrates the village into the money economy, and swallows much of the available cash. It is true that modern transportation does incorporate a region into the world market. It also trains the inhabitants for the consumption of foreign goods and the acceptance of foreign values. For example, throughout history Thailand was known for its klongs. These canals crisscrossed the country; people, rice, and tax collectors all moved easily along them. Some villages were cut off during the dry season, but their seasonal rhythm of life turned this periodic isolation into an occasion for meditation and festivities. A society that can afford long holidays and fill them with activities is certainly not poor. During the last half-decade major klongs were filled in to build roads. Since bus drivers are paid by the number of miles they can cover in a day, and since cars are still few, the Thais for a short while will be able to circulate in their country at world-record bus speeds. They will pay with the destruction of waterways that took millennia to build. The economists argue that buses and trucks pump more money per year through the economy. They do, but at the cost of depriving most Thais of the independence which their sleek rice boats once granted each family. Of course, car owners could never have competed with rice boats unless the World Bank had financed roads for them and the Thai government had made new laws that permitted them to profane the klongs.

The building trades are another example of an industry that modern nation-states impose on their societies, thereby modernizing the poverty of their citizens. The legal protection and financial support granted the industry reduces and cancels opportunities for the otherwise much more efficient self-builder. Quite recently Mexico launched a major program with the aim of providing all workers with proper housing. As a first step, new standards were set for the construction of dwelling units. These standards were intended to protect the little man who purchases a house from exploitation by the industry producing it. Paradoxically, these same standards deprived many more people of the traditional opportunity to house themselves. The code specifies minimum requirements that a man who builds his own house in his spare time cannot meet. Besides that, the real rent for industrially built quarters is more than the total income of 80 percent of the people. "Better housing," then, can be occupied only by those who are well-off or by those on whom the law bestows direct rent subsidies.

Once dwellings that fall below industrial standards are defined as improper, public funds are denied to the overwhelming majority of people who cannot buy housing but could "house" themselves. The tax funds meant to improve the living quarters of the poor are monopolized for the building of new towns next to the provincial and regional capitals where government employees, unionized workers, and people with good connections can live. These are all people who are employed in the modern sector of the economy, that is, people who *hold* jobs. They can be easily distinguished from other Mexicans because they have learned to speak about their *trabajo* as a noun, while the unemployed or the occasionally employed or those who live near the subsistence level do not use the noun form when they go to work.

These people, who *have* work, not only get subsidies for the building of their homes; the entire public-service sector is rearranged and developed to serve them. In Mexico City it has been estimated that 10 percent of the people use 50 percent of the household water, and on the high plain water is very scarce indeed. The building code has standards far below those of rich countries, but by prescribing certain ways in which houses must be built, it creates a rising scarcity of housing. The pretense of a society to provide ever better housing is the same kind of aberration we have met in the pretense of doctors to provide better health and of engineers to provide higher speeds. The setting of abstract impossible goals turns the means by which these are to be achieved into ends.

What happened in Mexico happened all over Latin America during the decade of the Alliance for Progress, including Cuba under Castro. It also happened in Massachusetts. In 1945, 32 percent of all one-family housing units in Massachusetts were still self-built: either built by their owners from foundation to roof or constructed under the full responsibility of the owner. By 1970 the proportion had gone down to 11 percent. Meanwhile, *housing* had been discovered as a major *problem*. The technological capability to produce tools and materials that favor self-building had increased in the intervening decades, but social arrangements—like unions, codes, mortgage rules, and markets—had turned against this choice.

Most people do not feel at home unless a significant proportion of the value of their houses is the result of the input of their own labor. Convivial policies would define what people who want to house themselves cannot get, and thereby make sure that all can get access to some minimum of physical space, to water, some basic building elements, some convivial tools ranging from power drills to mechanized pushcarts, and, probably, to some limited credit. Such an inversion of the present policy could give a postindustrial society modern homes almost as desirable for its members as those which were standard for the old Mayas and are still the rule in Yucatán.

Our present tools are engineered to deliver professional

energies. Such energies come in quanta. Less than a quantum cannot be delivered. Less than four years of schooling is worse than none. It only defines the former pupil as a dropout. This is equally true in medicine, transportation, and housing, as in agriculture and in the administration of justice. Mechanical transportation is worthwhile only at certain speeds. Conflict resolution is effective only when the issue is of sufficient weight to justify the costs of court action. The planting of new grains is productive only if the acreage and capital of the farmer are beyond a certain size. Powerful tools created to achieve abstractly conceived social goals inevitably deliver their output in quanta that are beyond the reach of a majority. What is more, these tools are integrated. Access to key positions in government or industry is reserved to those who are certified consumers of high quanta of schooling. They are the individuals chosen to run the plantation of mutant rubber trees, and they need a car to rush from meeting to meeting. Productivity demands the output of packaged quanta of institutionally defined values, and productive management demands the access of an individual to all these packages at once.

Professional goal-setting produces goods for an environment produced by other professions. Life that depends on high speed and apartment houses makes hospitals inevitable. By definition all these are scarce, and get even scarcer as they approach the standards set more recently by an ever-evolving profession; thereby each unit or quantum appearing on the market frustrates more people than it satisfies.

A just society would be one in which liberty for one person is constrained only by the demands created by equal liberty for another. Such a society requires as a precondition an agreement excluding tools that by their very nature prevent such liberty. This is true for tools that are fundamentally purely social arrangements, such as the school system, as well as for tools that are physical machines. In a convivial society compulsory and open-ended schooling would have to be excluded for the sake of justice. Age-specific, compulsory competition on an unending ladder for life-long privileges cannot increase equality but must favor those who start earlier, or who are healthier, or who are better equipped outside the classroom. Inevitably, it organizes society into many layers of failure, with each layer inhabited by dropouts schooled to believe that those who have consumed more education deserve more privilege because they are more valuable assets to society as a whole. A society constructed so that education by means of schools is a necessity for its functioning cannot be a just society. Power tools having certain structural characteristics are inevitably manipulative and must also be eliminated for the sake of justice. In a modern society, energy inputs represent one of the major new liberties. Each man's ability to produce change depends on his ability to control low-entropy energy. On this control of energy depends his right to give his meaning to the physical environment. His ability to act toward the future he chooses depends on his control of the energy that gives shape to that future. Equal freedom in a society that uses large amounts of environmental energy means equal control over the transformation of that energy and not just an equal claim to what has been done with it.

Most of the power tools now in use favor centralization of control. Industrial plants with their highly specialized tools give neither the worker nor most engineers a choice over what use will be made of the energy they manage. This is equally true, though less evident, of the high-powered consumer tools that dominate our society. Most of them, such as cars and air conditioners, are too costly to be available on an equal basis outside a few superrich societies. Others, such as mechanical household devices, are so specialized in nature that they in no way offer more freedom than much simpler hand tools. The monopoly of industrial production deprives even privileged clients of control over what they may get. Few people get the cars that most people want, and GM designers can only build vehicles to fit the existing roads.

Nations and multinational corporations have become

means for the spreading empire of international professions. Professional imperialism triumphs even where political and economic domination has been broken. Schools
everywhere are governed by pedagogues who read the same
books on learning theory and curriculum-planning. In a
given year, schools produce more or less the same model of
pupils in every nation. Nineteen-fifty graduates are as obsolete in Dakar as they are in Paris. The same iatrogenic
sicknesses are produced all over the world by doctors who
administer chloromycin or steroid pills. Every country
tends to select those productive processes which are more
capital-intensive and promise greater cost-benefit ratios,
so that the same kind of technological unemployment is
produced everywhere. Basic needs are defined as those that
international professions can meet. Since the local production of these wares is to the advantage of highly schooled
national elites, a country's doctors, teachers, and engineers
will defend it as an antidote to foreign domination. The
knowledge-capitalism of professional imperialism subju-
gates people more imperceptibly than and as effectively as
international finance or weaponry.

The principal source of injustice in our epoch is political
approval for the existence of tools that by their very nature
restrict to a very few the liberty to use them in an autonomous way. The pompous rituals by which each man is given
a vote to choose between factions only cover up the fact
that the imperialism of industrial tools is both arbitrary
and growing. Statistics which prove increased outputs and
high per capita consumption of professionally defined
quanta only veil the enormously high invisible costs. People get better education, better health, better transportation, better entertainment, and often even better nourishment only if the experts' goals are taken as the measurement
of what "better" means. The possibility of a convivial
society depends therefore on a new consensus about the destructiveness of imperialism on three levels: the pernicious
spread of one nation beyond its boundaries; the omni-
present influence of multinational corporations; and the

mushrooming of professional monopolies over production. Politics for convivial reconstruction of society must especially face imperialism on this third level, where it takes the form of professionalism. The public ownership of resources and of the means of production, and public control over the market and over net transfers of power, must be complemented by a public determination of the tolerable basic structure of modern tools. This means that politics in a postindustrial society must be mainly concerned with the development of design criteria for tools rather than as now with the choice of production goals. These politics would mean a structural inversion of the institutions now providing and defining new manmade essentials.

To invert politics, it will not be enough to show that a convivial life style is possible, or even to demonstrate that it is more attractive than life in a society ruled by industrial productivity. We cannot rest with the claim that this inversion would bring society closer to meeting the goals now stated as those of our major institutions. It is not even enough to show that a just or socially equal order can become a reality only through a convivial reconstruction of tools and the consequent redefinition of ownership and power. We need a way to recognize that the inversion of present political purpose is necessary for the survival of all people.

Most people have staked their self-images in the present structure and are unwilling to lose their ground. They have found security in one of the several ideologies that support further industrialization. They feel compelled to push the illusion of progress on which they are hooked. They long for and expect increased satisfaction, with less input of human energy and with more division of competence. They value handicraft and personal care as luxuries, but the ideal of a more labor-intensive, yet modern, production process seems to them quixotic and anachronistic.

It seems absurd to prepare politicians who have pledged themselves to increased outputs and better distribution of goods and services among their constituents for the day when a majority of voters will choose limits for all rather than promises of equal consumption. It appears equally hopeless to expect inverse insight from humanitarian liberals who have come to feel that feeding the starving millions is their vocation. They forget that people *eat,* and that people die when they are *fed.* These self-appointed keepers of their brothers make other people's survival depend on their own growing efficiency. By shifting from the production of guns to the production of grains they reduce their sense of guilt and increase their sense of power. They are blind to the convergence of population growth and the failure of the green revolution, which guarantees that feeding people now will escalate starvation by 1985. Their hubris distracts them from understanding that only the renunciation of industrial expansion can bring food and population into a balance in the so-called backward countries. The attempt to feed people and to control their increase are two mutually reinforcing, and very dangerous, illusions. Nor can economists foresee institutional inversion when for them all institutions must be evaluated according to the increase in their planned output and their ability to externalize internal diseconomics in an unobtrusive way. The terms and frameworks of economics have been shaped by the ideology of an irresistible institutionalization of values that overarches otherwise opposed economic creeds.

To translate the theoretical possibility of a postindustrial convivial life style into a political program for new tools, it must soon be shown that the prevailing fundamental structure of our present tools menaces the survival of mankind. It must be shown that this menace is imminent and that the effects of compulsive efficiency do more damage than good to most people in our generation. For this purpose we must identify the range within which our present institutions have become frustrating, and we must recognize another range within which our tools become destructive of society as a whole.

III

The Multiple Balance

The human equilibrium is open. It is capable of shifting within flexible but finite parameters. People can change, but only within bounds. In contrast, the present industrial system is dynamically unstable. It is organized for indefinite expansion and the concurrent unlimited creation of new needs, which in an industrial environment soon become basic necessities.

Once the industrial mode of production has become dominant in a society, it may still admit shifts from one type of output to another, but it does not admit limits to the further institutionalization of values. Such growth makes the incongruous demand that man seek his satisfaction by submitting to the logic of his tools.

The demands made by tools on people become increasingly costly. This rising cost of fitting man to the service of his tools is reflected in the ongoing shift from goods to services in over-all production. Increasing manipulation of man becomes necessary to overcome the resistance of his vital equilibrium to the dynamic of growing industries; it takes the form of educational, medical, and administrative therapies. Education turns out competitive consumers; medicine keeps them alive in the engineered environment they have come to require; bureaucracy reflects the necessity of exercising social control over people to do meaningless work. The parallel increase in the cost of the defense of new levels of privilege through: military, police, and insurance measures reflects the fact that in a consumer society there are inevitably two kinds of slaves: the prisoners of addiction and the prisoners of envy.

Political debate must now be focused on the various ways in which unlimited production threatens human life. This political debate will be misled by those who insist on prescribing palliatives which only disguise the deep reasons why the systems of health, transport, education, housing, and even politics and law are not working. The environmental crisis, for example, is rendered superficial if it is not pointed out that antipollution devices can only be effective if the total output of production decreases. Otherwise they tend to shift garbage out of sight, push it into the future, or dump it onto the poor. The total removal of the pollution created locally by a large-scale industry requires equipment, material, and energy that can create several times the damage elsewhere. Making antipollution devices compulsory only increases the unit cost of the product. This may conserve some fresh air for all, because fewer people can afford to drive cars or sleep in air-conditioned homes or fly to a fishing ground on the weekend, but it replaces damage to the physical environment with further social disintegration. To shift from coal to atomic power replaces smog now with higher radiation levels tomorrow. To relocate refineries overseas, where pollution controls are less stringent, preserves Americans—not Venezuelans—from unpleasant odors at the cost of higher levels of worldwide poisoning.

The overgrowth of tools threatens persons in ways which are profoundly new, though they are also analogous to traditional forms of nuisance and tort. These threats are of a new kind, because their perpetrators and victims are the same people: both operators and clients of inexorably destructive tools. Though some people may cash in on the game at first, ultimately all lose everything they have.

I will identify six ways in which all people of the world are threatened by industrial development after passage through the second watershed: (1) Overgrowth threatens the right to the fundamental physical structure of the environment with which man has evolved. (2) Industrialization threatens the right to convivial work. (3) The overprogramming of man for the new environment deadens his creative imagination. (4) New levels of productivity threaten the right to participatory politics. (5) Enforced obsolescence threatens the right to tradition: the recourse to precedent in language, myth, morals, and judgment. I will describe these five threats as distinct though interrelated categories all having in common a destructive inversion of means into ends. (6) Pervasive frustration by means of compulsory though engineered satisfaction constitutes a sixth and more subtle threat.

I am typifying the hazards created by the overgrowth of tools in six categories chosen so the damages can be recognized in traditional terms. That impersonal tools placed at the service of the injured party should inevitably inflict the injury is new, but the damage which threatens each person is not. These six categories can serve in the recovery of procedural principles by which people can expose and redress the present imbalance in the functioning of tools. These underlying principles of moral, political, and juridical procedure I assume to be three: recognition of the legitimacy of personal conflict, the dialectic authority of history over present procedures, and the recourse to laymen or peers for binding policy decisions. The radical functional inversion of our major institutions constitutes a revolution much more profound than the shifts in ownership or power usually proposed. It can be neither envisaged nor enacted unless a basic structure of procedure is recovered and clearly agreed upon. This structure can even now be discussed in concrete terms. I will therefore refer to formal juristic concepts in illustrating my argument.

1. Biological Degradation

The precarious balance between man and the biosphere has been recognized and has suddenly begun to worry many people. The degradation of the environment is dramatic and highly visible. For years car traffic in Mexico City increased steadily under a sparkling sky. Then, within a couple of years, smog descended and soon became worse than in Los Angeles. This phenomenon can be easily discussed and appreciated by people who have never studied science. Poisons of unknown potency are discharged into the biotic system of the earth. There is no way to retrieve some of them, nor any means to predict how some of them may suddenly combine their action so that the whole earth, like Lake Erie or Baikal, will die. Man has evolved to fit into one niche in the universe. The earth is his home. This home is now threatened by the impact of man.

Overpopulation, excessive affluence, and faulty technology are usually identified as the three trends which combine and threaten to break the environmental balance. Paul Ehrlich points out that to face honestly the need for population control and stabilized consumption may "expose one to the painful criticism of being both anti-people and anti-poor," but he also emphasizes that "these unpopular measures offer mankind's only hope for averting unprecedented misery." Ehrlich wants to implement birth control with industrial efficiency. Barry Commoner insists that faulty technology, the third element in the equation, accounts for most of the recent deterioration in the quality of the environment. He exposes himself to the criticism of being an antitechnological demagogue. Commoner wants to retool industry rather than invert the basic structure of our tools.

Fascination with the environmental crisis has forced the debate about survival to focus on only one balance threatened by tools. A one-dimensional dispute is futile. Three trends have indeed been identified, each of them tending to upset the balance between man and the physical environment. Overpopulation makes more people dependent on limited resources. Affluence compels each person to use more energy. Faulty technology degrades energy in an inefficient way.

If these three trends are considered to be the only significant threats, and the physical environment is considered as the only fundamental milieu that is threatened, only two central issues must be discussed: (1) To decide which factor or trend has degraded the environment most, and which factor will impose the greatest burden on the environment during the next few years. (2) To decide which factor merits most attention because we can in some way reduce or invert it. One party claims it is easier to do away with people, the other that it is more feasible to reduce entropy-producing production.

Honesty requires that we each recognize the need to limit procreation, consumption, and waste, but equally we must radically reduce our expectations that machines will do our work for us or that therapists can make us learned or healthy. The only solution to the environmental crisis is the shared insight of people that they would be happier if they could *work* together and *care* for each other. Such an inversion of the current world view requires intellectual courage for it exposes us to the unenlightened yet painful criticism of being not only antipeople and against economic progress, but equally against liberal education and scientific and technological advance. We must face the fact that the imbalance between man and the environment is just one of several mutually reinforcing stresses, each distorting the balance of life in a different dimension. In this view, overpopulation is the result of a distortion in the balance of learning, dependence on affluence is the result of a radical monopoly of institutional over personal values, and faulty technology is inexorably consequent upon a transformation of means into ends.

The one-dimensional debate among proponents of various panaceas for the ecological imbalance will only inspire the false expectation that somehow human action can be engineered to fit into the requirements of the world conceived as a technological totality. Bureaucratically guaranteed survival under such circumstances means the expansion of industrial economics to the point where a centrally planned system of production and reproduction is identified with the guided evolution of the Earth. If such an industrially minded solution becomes generally accepted as the only way of preserving a viable environment, the preservation of the physical milieu can become the rationale for a bureaucratic Leviathan at the levers which regulate levels of human reproduction, expectation, production, and consumption. Such a technological response to growing population, pollution, and affluence can be founded only on a further development of the presently prevailing institutionalization of values. The belief in the possibility of this development is founded on an erroneous supposition, namely, that "The historical achievement of science and technology has rendered possible the *translation of values into technical tasks*—the materialization of values. Consequently, what is at stake is the redefinition of values in *technical terms,* as elements in technological process. The new ends, as technical ends, would then operate in the project and in the construction of the machinery, and not only in its utilization." *

The re-establishment of an ecological balance depends on the ability of society to counteract the progressive materialization of values. Otherwise man will find himself totally enclosed within his artificial creation, with no exit. Enveloped in a physical, social, and psychological milieu of his own making, he will be a prisoner in the shell of technology, unable to find again the ancient milieu to which he was adapted for hundreds of thousands of years. The ecological balance cannot be re-established unless we recognize again that only persons have ends and that only persons can work toward them. Machines only operate ruthlessly to reduce people to the role of impotent allies in their destructive progress.

2. Radical Monopoly

When overefficient tools are applied to facilitate man's relations with the physical environment, they can destroy the balance between man and nature. Overefficient tools

* Herbert Marcuse, *One-Dimensional Man*, Boston, 1970.

corrupt the environment. But tools can also be made over-efficient in quite a different way. They can upset the relationship between what people need to do by themselves and what they need to obtain ready-made. In this second dimension overefficient production results in radical monopoly.

By radical monopoly I mean a kind of dominance by one product that goes far beyond what the concept of monopoly usually implies. Generally we mean by "monopoly" the exclusive control by one corporation over the means of producing (or selling) a commodity or service. Coca-Cola can create a monopoly over the soft-drink market in Nicaragua by being the only maker of soft drinks which advertises with modern means. Nestlé might impose its brand of cocoa by controlling the raw material, some car maker by restricting imports of other makes, a television channel by licensing. Monopolies of this kind have been recognized for a century as dangerous by-products of industrial expansion, and legal devices have been developed in a largely futile attempt to control them. Monopolies of this kind restrict the choices open to the consumer. They might even compel him to buy one product on the market, but they seldom simultaneously abridge his liberties in other domains. A thirsty man might desire a cold, gaseous, and sweet drink and find himself restricted to the choice of just one brand. He still remains free to quench his thirst with beer or water. Only if and when his thirst is translated without meaningful alternatives into the need for a Coke would the monopoly become radical. By "radical monopoly" I mean the dominance of one type of product rather than the dominance of one brand. I speak about radical monopoly when one industrial production process exercises an exclusive control over the satisfaction of a pressing need, and excludes nonindustrial activities from competition.

Cars can thus monopolize traffic. They can shape a city into their image—practically ruling out locomotion on foot or by bicycle in Los Angeles. They can eliminate river traffic in Thailand. That motor traffic curtails the right to walk, not that more people drive Chevies than Fords, constitutes radical monopoly. What cars do to people by virtue of this radical monopoly is quite distinct from and independent of what they do by burning gasoline that could be transformed into food in a crowded world. It is also distinct from automotive manslaughter. Of course cars burn gasoline that could be used to make food. Of course they are dangerous and costly. But the radical monopoly cars establish is destructive in a special way. Cars create distance. Speedy vehicles of all kinds render space scarce. They drive wedges of highways into populated areas, and then extort tolls on the bridge over the remoteness between people that was manufactured for their sake. This monopoly over land turns space into car fodder. It destroys the environment for feet and bicycles. Even if planes and buses could run as nonpolluting, nondepleting public services, their inhuman velocities would degrade man's innate mobility and force him to spend more time for the sake of travel.

Schools tried to extend a radical monopoly on learning by redefining it as education. As long as people accepted the teacher's definition of reality, those who learned outside school were officially stamped "uneducated." Modern medicine deprives the ailing of care not prescribed by doctors. Radical monopoly exists where a major tool rules out natural competence. Radical monopoly imposes compulsory consumption and thereby restricts personal autonomy. It constitutes a special kind of social control because it is enforced by means of the imposed consumption of a standard product that only large institutions can provide.

The control of undertakers over burial shows how radical monopoly functions and how it differs from other forms of culturally defined behavior. A generation ago, in Mexico, only the opening of the grave and the blessing of the dead body were performed by professionals: the gravedigger and the priest. A death in the family created various demands, all of which could be taken care of within the family. The wake, the funeral, and the dinner served to compose quarrels, to vent grief, and to remind each participant of the fatality of death and the value of life. Most of these were of a ritual nature and carefully prescribed—different from region to region. Recently, funeral homes were established in the major cities. At first undertakers had difficulty finding clients because even in large cities people still knew how to bury their dead. During the sixties the funeral homes obtained control over new cemeteries and began offering package deals, including the casket, church service, and embalming. Now legislation is being passed to make the mortician's ministrations compulsory. Once he gets hold of the body, the funeral director will have established a radical monopoly over burial, as medicine is at the point of establishing one over dying.

The current debate over health-care delivery in the United States clearly illustrates the entrenchment of a radical monopoly. Each political party in the debate makes sick care a burning public issue and thereby relegates health care to an area about which politics has nothing important to say. Each party promises more funds to doctors, hospitals, and drugstores. Such promises are not in the interest of the majority. They only serve to increase the power of a minority of professionals to prescribe the tools men are to use in maintaining health, healing sickness, and repressing death. More funds will strengthen the hold of the health industry over public resources and heighten its prestige and arbitrary power. Such power in the hands of a minority will produce only an increase in suffering and a decrease in personal self-reliance. More money will be invested in tools that only postpone unavoidable death and in services that abridge even further the civil rights of those who want to heal each other. More money spent under the control of the health profession means that more people are operationally conditioned into playing the role of the sick, a role they are not allowed to interpret for themselves. Once they accept this role, their most trivial needs can be satisfied only through commodities that are scarce by professional definition.

People have a native capacity for healing, consoling, moving, learning, building their houses, and burying their dead. Each of these capacities meets a need. The means for the satisfaction of these needs are abundant so long as they depend primarily on what people can do for themselves, with only marginal dependence on commodities. These activities have use-value without having been given exchange-value. Their exercise at the service of man is not considered labor.

These basic satisfactions become scarce when the social environment is transformed in such a manner that basic needs can no longer be met by abundant competence. The establishment of radical monopoly happens when people give up their native ability to do what they can do for themselves and for each other, in exchange for something "better" that can be done for them only by a major tool. Radical monopoly reflects the industrial institutionalization of values. It substitutes the standard package for the personal response. It introduces new classes of scarcity and a new device to classify people according to the level of their consumption. This redefinition raises the unit cost of valuable service, differentially rations privilege, restricts access to resources, and makes people dependent. Above all, by depriving people of the ability to satisfy personal needs in a personal manner, radical monopoly creates radical scarcity of personal—as opposed to institutional—service.

Against this radical monopoly people need protection. They need this protection whether consumption is imposed by the private interests of undertakers, by the government for the sake of hygiene, or by the self-destructive collusion between the mortician and the survivors, who want to do the best thing for their dear departed. They need this protection even if the majority is now sold on the professional's services. Unless the need for protection from radical monopoly is recognized, its multiple implementation can break the tolerance of man for enforced inactivity and passivity.

It is not always easy to determine what constitutes com-

pulsory consumption. The monopoly held by schools is
not established primarily by a law that threatens punishment to parent or child for truancy. Such laws exist, but
school is established by other tactics: by discrimination
against the unschooled, by centralizing learning tools under the control of teachers, by restricting public funds ear-
marked for baby-sitting to salaries for graduates from
normal schools. Protection against laws that impose education, vaccination, or life prolongation is important, but it
is not sufficient. Procedures must be used that permit any
party who feels threatened by compulsory consumption to
claim protection, whatever form the imposition takes. Like
intolerable pollution, intolerable monopoly cannot be defined in advance. The threat can be anticipated, but the
definition of its precise nature can result only from people's
participation in deciding what may not be produced.

Protection against this general monopoly is as difficult
as protection against pollution. People will face a danger
that threatens their own self-interest but not one that threatens society as a whole. Many more people are against cars
than are against driving them. They are against cars because they pollute and because they monopolize traffic.
They drive cars because they consider the pollution created
by one car insignificant, and because they do not feel person-
ally deprived of freedom when they drive. It is also difficult
to be protected against monopoly when a society is already
littered with roads, schools, or hospitals, when independent
action has been paralyzed for so long that the ability for it
seems to have atrophied, and when simple alternatives
seem beyond the reach of the imagination. Monopoly is
hard to get rid of when it has frozen not only the shape of
the physical world but also the range of behavior and of
imagination. Radical monopoly is generally discovered only
when it is too late.

Commercial monopoly is broken at the cost of the few
who profit from it. Usually, these few manage to evade controls. The cost of radical monopoly is already borne by the
public and will be broken only if the public realizes that

it would be better off paying the costs of ending the monopoly than by continuing to pay for its maintenance. But the price will not be paid unless the public learns to value the potential of a convivial society over the illusion of progress. It will not be paid voluntarily by those who confuse conviviality with intolerable poverty.

Some of the symptoms of radical monopoly are reaching public awareness, above all the degree to which frustration grows faster than output in even the most highly developed countries and under whatever political regime. Policies aimed to ease this frustration may easily distract attention from the general nature of the monopoly at its roots, however. The more these reforms succeed in correcting superficial abuses, the better they serve to bolster the monopoly I am trying to describe.

The first palliative is consumer protection. Consumers cannot do without cars. They buy different makes. They discover that most cars are unsafe at any speed. So they organize to get safer, better, and more durable cars and to get more as well as wider and safer roads. Yet when consumers gain more confidence in cars, the victory only increases society's dependence on high-powered vehicles—public or private—and frustrates even more those who have to, or would prefer to, walk.

While the organized self-protection of the addict-consumer immediately raises the quality of the dope and the power of the peddler, it also may lead ultimately to limits on growth. Cars may finally become too expensive to purchase and medicines too expensive to test. By exacerbating the contradictions inherent in this institutionalization of values, majorities can more easily become aware of them. Discerning consumers who are discriminatory in their purchasing habits may finally discover that they can do better by doing things for themselves.

The second palliative proposed to cure growing frustration with growing output is planning. The illusion is common that planners with socialist ideals might somehow create a socialist society in which industrial workers constitute a majority. The proponents of this idea overlook the fact that anticonvivial and manipulative tools can fit into a socialist society in only a very limited measure. Once transportation, education, or medicine is offered by a government free of cost, its use can be enforced by moral guardians. The underconsumer can be blamed for sabotage of the national effort. In a market economy, someone who wants to cure his flu by staying in bed will be penalized only through loss of income. In a society that appeals to the "people" to meet centrally determined production goals, resistance to the consumption of medicine becomes an act of public immorality. Protection against radical monopoly depends on a political consensus opposed to growth. Such a consensus is diametrically opposed to the issues now raised by political oppositions, since these converge in the demand to increase growth and to provide more and better things for more completely disabled people.

Both the balance that defines man's need for a hospitable environment and the balance that defines everyone's need for authentic activity are now close to the breaking point. And still this danger does not concern most people. It must now be explained why most people are either blind to this threat or feel helpless to correct it. I believe that the blindness is due to the decline in a third balance—the balance of learning—and that the impotence people experience is the result of yet a fourth upset in what I call the balance of power.

3. Overprogramming

The balance of learning is determined by the ratio of two kinds of knowledge in a society. The first is a result of the creative action of people on their environment, and the second represents the result of man's "trivialization" by his manufactured milieu. Their first kind of knowledge is derived from the primary involvement of people with each other and from their use of convivial tools; the second accrues to them as a result of purposeful and programmed training to which they are subjected. Speaking the mother tongue is learned in the first way, while some pupils learn mathematics in the second. No sane person would say that speaking or walking or nursing a child is primarily the result of education, while competence in mathematics, ballet dancing, or painting usually is.

The relation between what can be learned from ordinary living and what must be learned as a result of intentional teaching differs widely with place and time. It depends very much on rituals. All Muslims learn some Arabic as the result of prayer. This learning evolves from interaction in a context bounded by tradition. In much the same manner, peasants pick up the folklore of their region. Class and caste also generate opportunities to learn. The rich acquire "proper" table manners or accents and insist that these cannot be taught. The poor learn to fend in dignity where no education could teach the rich to survive.

Crucial to how much anyone can learn on his own is the structure of his tools: the less they are convivial, the more they foster teaching. In limited and well-integrated tribes, knowledge is shared quite equally among most members. All people know most of what everybody knows. On a higher level of civilization, new tools are introduced; more people know more things, but not all know how to execute them equally well. Mastery of skill does not yet imply a monopoly of understanding. One can understand fully what a goldsmith does without being one oneself. Men do not have to be cooks to know how to prepare food. This combination of widely shared information and competence for using it is characteristic of a society in which convivial tools prevail. The techniques used are easily understood by observing the artisan at work, but the skills employed are complex and usually can be acquired only through lengthy and programmed apprenticeship. Total learning expands when the range of spontaneous learning widens along with access to an increasing number of taught skills and both liberty and discipline flower. This expansion of the balance of learning cannot go on forever; it is self-limiting. It can be optimized, but it cannot be forcibly extended. One reason is that man's life span is limited. Another—just as inexorable—is that the specialization of tools and the division of labor reinforce each other. When centralization and specialization grow beyond a certain point, they require highly programmed operators and clients. More of what each man must know is due to what another man has designed and has the power to force on him.

The city child is born into an environment made up of systems that have a different meaning for their designers than for their clients. The inhabitant of the city is in touch with thousands of systems, but only peripherally with each. He knows how to operate the TV or the telephone, but their workings are hidden from him. Learning by primary experience is restricted to self-adjustment in the midst of packaged commodities. He feels less and less secure in doing his own thing. Cooking, courtesy, and sex become subject matters in which instruction is required. The balance of learning deteriorates: it is skewed in favor of "education." People know what they have been taught, but learn little from their own doing. People come to feel that they need "education."

Learning thus becomes a commodity, and, like any commodity that is marketed, it becomes scarce. The nature of this scarcity is hidden—at a high cost—by the many forms education takes. Education can be programmed preparation *for* life in the future in the form of packaged, serial instructions produced by schools, or it can be constant communication *about* ongoing life through the output of the media and through the instructions built into consumer goods. Sometimes these instructions are attached to the item and must be read. In more thoroughly designed goods, the shape, color, and provoked associations speak to the user about the way the item must be handled. Education can also become a periodic remedy for workers whose original training gets left behind by industrial innovation. When people become obsolete and need constantly to renew their educational security, when the accountant must be repro-

grammed for each new generation of computers, then learning has indeed become scarce. Education becomes the most
vulnerable and confusing issue in the society.

Everywhere the direct cost of training rises faster than
the total output. This has been interpreted in either of
two ways. One interpretation assumes that education is a
means to a social end. From this perspective the capitaliza-
tion of man through knowledge inputs is a necessary requirement for higher productivity. The disproportionate
growth rate of the educational sector means total production is nearing an asymptote. To avoid this, ways must be
found to increase the cost-benefit ratio in education.
Schools will be the first victims of a drive for rationalization in the production of knowledge capital. In my opinion,
this is unfortunate. Although the school is destructive and
quite inefficient, its traditional character protects at least
some rights of the pupil. Educators freed from the restraint
of schools could be much more effective and deadly conditioners.

The second interpretation starts from the opposite assumption. According to this view, education is the most
valuable output of institutional growth. The transition to a
stationary state in the production of goods and perhaps
even of energy will usher in an explosive growth in the production of invisible commodities such as information, education, and fun. In this argument the marginal utility of
education also decreases, but this is no reason to limit its
production. Some economists go even further. In the name
of a misnamed quality of life they want to put the brakes
on the manufacturing sector when it interferes with the
growth of the service sector, seemingly unaware of the stulti-
fying effects of escalating treatments. In neither of these two
views is a distinction made between learning by the use
of convivial tools and learning through manipulation.
Both views skew the balance of learning by increasing manipulative teaching and crushing autonomous questions.
Those who treat education as a means for production and
those who treat education as the supreme luxury product

agree on the need for more education. They upset the balance of learning in favor of more teaching. They assume that a modern world is inevitably so alien that it has passed beyond the reach of people and can be known only by mystagogues and disciples.

The transformation of learning into education paralyzes man's poetic ability, his power to endow the world with his personal meaning. Man will wither away just as much if he is deprived of nature, of his own work, or of his deep need to learn what he wants and not what others have planned that he should learn. The overdetermination of the physical environment renders it hostile. Radical monopoly makes people prisoners of welfare. Men overwhelmed by commodities are rendered impotent and in their rage either kill or die. The corruption of the balance of learning makes people into puppets of their tools.

Poets and clowns have always risen up against the oppression of creative thought by dogma. They expose literal-mindedness with metaphor. They demonstrate the follies of seriousness in a framework of humor. Their intimate wonder dissolves certainties, banishes fears, and undoes paralysis. The prophet can denounce creeds and expose superstitions and mobilize persons to use their lights and wits. Poetry, intuition, and theory can offer intimations of the advance of dogma against wit that may lead to a revolution in awareness. Only the separation of church and state, of compulsory knowledge from political action, can redress the balance of learning. The law has been used, and can be used again, to this purpose. The law has protected societies against the exaggerated claims of its priests, and can protect it against the claims of educators. Compulsory school attendance or other compulsory treatment is analogous to compulsory attendance at a religious ritual. The law can disestablish it. The law can be used against the rising cost of education, and against the use of education in the reproduction of a class society.

To understand the rising cost of education, we must recognize two facts: first, that nonconvivial tools create educational side effects which at some point become intolerable and, second, that education which employs nonconvivial tools is economically unfeasible. The first recognition opens our eyes to the possibility of a society where work and leisure and politics would favor learning and that could function with less formal education; the second recognition permits us to set up educational arrangements that favor self-initiated, self-chosen learning, and that relegate programmed teaching to limited, clearly specified occasions.

Throughout the world, highly capitalized tools require highly capitalized men. Following the Second World War, economic development penetrated even "backward" areas. Spot industrialization created an intense demand for schools to program people not only to operate but also to live with their new tools. The establishment of more schools in Malaysia or Brazil teaches people the accountant's view of the value of time, the bureaucrat's view of the value of promotion, the salesman's view of the value of increased consumption, and the union leader's view of the purpose of work. People are taught all this not by the teacher but by the curriculum hidden in the structure of school. It does not matter what the teacher teaches so long as the pupil has to attend hundreds of hours of age-specific assemblies to engage in a routine decreed by the curriculum and is graded according to his ability to submit it. People learn that they acquire more value in the market if they spend more hours in class. They learn to value progressive consumption of curricula. They learn that whatever a major institution produces has value, even invisible things such as education or health. They learn to value grade advancement, passive submission, and even the standard misbehavior that teachers like to interpret as a sign of creativity. They learn disciplined competition for the favor of the bureaucrat who presides over their daily sessions, who is called their teacher as long as they are in class and their boss when they go to work. They learn to define themselves as holders of knowledge stock in the specialty in which they have made investments of their time. They learn to accept their place in society precisely in the class and career corresponding to the level at which they leave school and to the field of their academic specialization.

Industrial jobs are arranged so that the better-schooled fit into the scarcer slots. Scarce jobs are defined as more productive, so people with less schooling are barred from access to the more desirable goods produced in the new industries. Industrially produced shoes, bags, clothes, frozen foods, and soft drinks drive off the market equivalent goods that had been convivially produced. As production becomes more centralized and more capital-intensive, the screening process performed by tax-supported schools not only costs more for those who get through it, but double-charges those who do not.

Education becomes necessary not only to grade people for jobs but to upgrade them for consumption. As industrial output rises, it pushes the education system to exercise the social control necessary for its efficient use. The housing industry in Latin-American countries is a good example of the educational diseconomies produced by architects. All the major cities in such countries are surrounded by vast tracts of self-built *favelas, barriadas,* or *poblaciones.* Components for new houses and utilities could be made very cheaply and designed for self-assembly. People could build more durable, more comfortable, and more sanitary dwellings, as well as learn about new materials and systems. But instead of supporting the ability of people to shape their own environment, the government deposits in these shanty-towns public utilities designed for people who live in standard modern houses. The presence of a new school, a paved road, and a glass-and-steel police station defines the professionally built house as the functional unit, and stamps the self-built home a shanty. The law establishes this definition by refusing a building permit to people who cannot submit a plan signed by an architect. People are deprived of their ability to invest their own time with the power to produce use-value, and are compelled to work for wages and to exchange their earnings for industrially defined rented space. They are deprived also of the opportunity to learn while building.

Industrial society demands that some people be taught before they can drive a truck and that other people be taught before they can build a house. Others must be taught how to live in apartment buildings. Teachers, social workers, and policemen cooperate to keep people who have low-paying or occasional jobs in houses they may not build or change. To accommodate more people on less land, Venezuela and Brazil experimented with high-rise tenements. First, the police had to dislodge people from their "slums" and resettle them in apartments. Then the social workers had to socialize tenants who lacked sufficient schooling to understand that pigs may not be raised on eleventh-floor balconies nor beans cultivated in their bathtubs.

In New York people with less than twelve years of schooling are treated like cripples: they tend to be unemployable, and are controlled by social workers who decide for them how to live. The radical monopoly of overefficient tools exacts from society the increasing and costly conditioning of clients. Ford produces cars that can be repaired only by trained mechanics. Agriculture departments turn out high-yield crops that can be used only with the assistance of farm managers who have survived an expensive school race. The production of better health, higher speeds, or greater yields depends on more disciplined recipients. The real cost of these doubtful benefits is hidden by unloading much of them on the schools that produce social control.

Pressure for more and better conditioning of people in the name of education has led schools over their second watershed. Planners make programs more varied and complex, but their marginal utility thereby declines. Compulsory attendance has been extended to the point that it now can be defined by teachers as independent study on the city streets, or as a field project supervised by the weavers of Teotitlán del Valle.

Parallel with the growing pretensions of school, other agencies discovered their educational mission. Newspapers, television, and radio were no longer just media of communication. They were pressed into the service of socialization. Periodicals expanded to accommodate all fit news, which meant that a few professional journalists got vast readerships, while the majority was reduced to token representation in the "Letters to the Editor" section.

The industrial manufacture and marketing of knowledge reduce the access of people to convivial tools for self-initiated learning. Witness the fate of the book. The book is the result of two major inventions that enormously extended the balance of learning: the alphabet and the printing press. Both techniques are almost ideally convivial. Almost anybody can learn to use them, and for his own purpose. They use cheap materials. People can take them or leave them as they wish. They are not easily controlled by third parties. Even the Soviet government cannot stop the *samizdat* circulation of subversive typescripts.

The alphabet and the printing press have in principle deprofessionalized the recorded word. With the alphabet the merchant broke the monopoly of the priest over hieroglyphs. With cheap paper and pencil, and later with the typewriter and modern copying devices, a set of new techniques had in principle opened the era of nonprofessional, truly convivial, communication by record. The tape recorder and camera added new media to fully interactive communication. Yet the manipulative nature of institutions and schooling for the acceptance of manipulation have put these ideally convivial tools at the service of more one-way teaching. Schools train people in the use of constantly revised textbooks. They produce readers of instructions and of news. The per capita purchase of nontechnical books by high school graduates declines with the increased percentage of people who finish high school. More books are written for the school-trained specialist, and the self-initiated reading of books declines. More people spend more time hooked on the curriculum defined by new principals: the publisher, the producer, and the program director. Every week they wait for *Time*.

Even the library has become a component of a schooled world. As the library got "better," the book was further withdrawn from the handy bookshelf. The reference librarian placed himself between people and shelves; now he is being replaced by the computer. Putting the book into huge deposits and into the hands of computers, the New York Public Library has become so expensive to operate that it now opens only from ten to six weekdays and is open only partially on Saturdays. This means that its books have become the specialized tool of readers who live on a grant to stay away from work and school.

At its best the library is the prototype of a convivial tool. Repositories for other learning tools can be organized on its model, expanding access to tapes, pictures, records, and very simple labs filled with the same scientific instruments with which most of the major breakthroughs of the last century were made.

Manipulative teaching tools raise the cost of learning. Now we only ask what people have to learn and then invest in a means to teach them. We should learn to ask first what people need if they want to learn and provide these tools for them. Professional teachers laugh at the idea that people would learn more from random access to learning resources than they can be taught. In fact, they frequently cite as proof for their skepticism the declining use of libraries. They overlook the fact that libraries are little used because they have been organized as formidable teaching devices. Libraries are not used because people have been trained to demand that they be taught. Neither are contraceptives, and for analogous reasons we have to explore.

People must learn to live within bounds. This cannot be *taught*. Survival depends on people *learning* fast what they *cannot* do. They must *learn* to abstain from unlimited progeny, consumption, and use. It is impossible to *educate* people for voluntary poverty or to manipulate them into self-control. It is impossible to *teach* joyful renunciation in a world totally structured for higher output and the illusion of declining costs.

People must learn why and how to practice contraception. The reason is clear. Man has evolved in a small corner of the universe. His world is bounded by the resources of the ecosphere, and can accommodate only a limited number of people. Technology has transformed the characteristics of this niche. The ecosphere now accommodates a larger number of people, each less vitally adapted to the environment—each on the average having less space, less freedom to survive with simple means, fewer roots in tradition. The attempt to make a better environment has turned out to be as presumptuous as the attempt to create better health, education, or communication. As a result there are now more people, most of them less at home in the world. This large population can survive because of new tools. In turn, it spurs the search for even more powerful tools, and thereby demands more radical monopoly; this monopoly, in its turn, calls for more and more education. But, paradoxically, what people most need to learn, they cannot be *taught* or *educated* to do. If they are voluntarily to keep their numbers and consumption without bounds, they must learn to do so by living active and responsible lives, or they will perish—passive though well informed, frustrated yet resigned. Voluntary and therefore effective population control is impossible under conditions of radical monopoly and overprogramming. An efficient, specialized birth control program must fail in the same way that schools and hospitals fail. It can start with a futile attempt at effective seduction. It will logically escalate to enforced sterilization and abortion. Finally, it will provide a rationale for megadeaths.

Voluntary and effective contraception is now absolutely necessary. If such contraception is not practiced in the very near future, humanity is in danger of being crushed by its own size rather than by the power of its tools. But this universal practice cannot possibly be the result of some miracle tool. A new practice, inverse to the present, can only be the result of a new relationship between people and their tools. The universal practice of effective contraception is a necessary premise for the limitation of tools which I advocate. But equally, the psychological inversion that will accompany a limitation of tools is a premise for the convivial psychological pressure necessary for effective contraception.

The devices needed for birth control are a paradigm for modern convivial tools. They incorporate science in instruments that can be handled by any reasonably prudent and well-apprenticed person. They provide new ways to engage in the millenary practice of contraception, sterilization, and abortion. They are cheap enough to be made universally available. They are made to fit alternate tasks, beliefs, and situations. They are obviously tools that structure the bodily relationship of each individual to himself and to others. To be effective, some must be used by every adult, and many of them must be used every day. Birth control is an immense task. It must be accomplished within one decade. It can be accomplished only in a convivial manner. It is ridiculous to try to control populations with tools which by their nature are convivial while conditioning the population by formal education to fit more effectively into an industrial and professional world. It is absurd to expect that Brazilian peasants can be taught to depend on doctors for injections and prescriptions, on lawyers for conflict resolution, and on teachers for learning to read, while asking them to use the condom on their own. But it is equally fanciful to expect that Indian doctors will allow illiterate but well-trained hospital assistants to compete with them in the performance of sterilizations. If the public realized that this delicate intervention could be equally or even more carefully performed by a layman whose attention, dexterity, and programming skills were refined in the weaving of saris, doctors would lose their monopoly on all interventions which are economically feasible for any majority of people. Professional taboos and industrial tools stand and fall together once truly rational, postindustrial tools are available. Only the convergent use of convivial tools in all significant areas of need-satisfaction can render their use in each sector truly effective. Only among convivially structured tools can people learn to use the new levels of power that modern technology can incorporate in them.

4. Polarization

The present organization of tools impels societies to grow both in population and in levels of affluence. This growth takes place at the opposite ends of the privilege spectrum. The underprivileged grow in number, while the already privileged grow in affluence. The underprivileged thus strengthen their frustrating claims, while the rich defend their presumed rights and needs. Hunger and impotence lead the poor to demand rapid industrialization, and the defense of growing luxuries pushes the rich into more frantic production. Power is polarized, frustration is generalized, and the alternative of greater happiness at lower affluences pushed into the blind spot of social vision.

This blindness is a result of the broken balance of learning. People who are hooked on teaching are conditioned to be customers for everything else. They see their own personal growth as an accumulation of institutional outputs, and prefer what institutions *make* over what they themselves can do. They repress the ability to discover reality by their own lights. The skewed balance of learning explains why the radical monopoly of commodities has become imperceptible. It does not explain why people feel impotent to correct those profound disorders which they do perceive.

This helplessness is the result of a fourth disruption: the growing polarization of power. Under the pressure of an expanding megamachine, power is concentrated in a few hands, and the majority becomes dependent on handouts. New levels of luxuriant overproduction grow faster than the output of commodities which this wanton production imposes.

A 3 percent increase in the standard of living of the U.S. population costs 25 times as much as a similar increase in the living standard of India, despite the greater size and more rapid growth of the Indian population. Significant benefits for the poor demand a reduction of the resources used by the rich, while significant benefits for the rich make murderous demands on the resources of the poor. Yet the rich pretend that by exploiting the poor nations they will become rich enough to create a hyperindustrial abundance for all. The elites of poor countries share this fantasy.

The rich will get richer and many more of the poor will become destitute during the next ten years. But anguish about the hungry should not prevent us from understanding the structural problem of power distribution that constitutes the fourth dimension of destructive overgrowth. Unchecked industrialization modernizes poverty. Poverty levels rise and the gap between rich and poor widens. These two aspects must be seen together or the nature of destructive polarization will be missed.

Poverty levels rise because industrial staples are turned into basic necessities and have a unit cost beyond what a majority could ever pay. The radical monopoly of industries has created new types of demeaning poverty in societies of sometimes profligate affluence. The former subsistence farmer is put out of business by the green revolution. He earns more as a laborer, but he cannot give his children their former diet. More importantly, the U.S. citizen with ten times his income is also desperately poor. Both get increasingly less at greater cost.

The other side of modernized poverty is related but distinct. The power gap widens because control over production is centralized to make the most goods for the greatest number. Whereas rising poverty levels are due to the structure of industrial outputs, the gaping power lag is due to the structure of inputs. To seek remedies for the former without simultaneously dealing with the latter would only postpone and aggravate the world-wide modernization of poverty.

The surface effects of industrially concentrated power can be obviated by income equalization. Progressive taxes without loopholes can be supplemented by social security, income supports, and equal welfare benefits for all. Confiscation of private capital beyond a certain limit can be attempted. Keeping maximum close to minimum income is an even tougher way to stem personal enrichment through the management of corporate power. But such curbs on personal income will be effective only in regulating private consumption. It has no effect on equalizing the privileges that really count in a society where the job has become more important than the home. As long as workers are graded by the amount of manpower capital they represent, those who hold high denominations of knowledge stock will be certified for the use of all kinds of timesaving privileges. The concentration of privileges on a few is in the nature of industrial dominance.

With the introduction of agriculture and animal husbandry, patriarchal government and some centralization of power became feasible. At this stage political means could be used to get the power of many slaves under one man's control. One man could transform a multitude into a tool for the realization of his design. Religion, ideology, and the whip were the principal means of control. But the amount of power controlled was small. The centralization of power which now seems normal could not have been imagined even a century ago.

In modern society, energy conversion enormously exceeds the body power of all men. Manpower stands to mechanical power in a ratio of 1:15 in China and 1:300 in the USA. Switches concentrate the control over this power more effectively than whips ever could. The social distribution of control over power inputs has been radically changed. If capital means the power to make effective change, power inflation has reduced most people to paupers.

As tools get bigger, the number of potential operators declines. There are always fewer operators of cranes than of wheelbarrows. As tools become more efficient, more scarce resources are put at the service of the operator. On a Guatemalan construction site, only the engineer gets air conditioning in his trailer. He is also the only one whose time is deemed so precious that he must be flown to the capital, and whose decisions seem so important that they are transmitted by shortwave radio. He has of course earned his privileges by cornering the largest amount of tax money and using it to acquire a university degree. The Indio who works on the gang does not notice the relative increase in privilege between him and his Ladino gang boss, but the geometricians and draftsmen who also went to school, but did not graduate, feel the heat and the distance from their families in a new and acute way. Their relative poverty has been aggravated by their bosses' claim to greater efficiency.

Never before have tools approached present power. Never before have they been so integrated at the service of a small elite. Kings could not claim divine right with as little challenge as executives claim services for the sake of greater production. The Russians justify supersonic transport by saying it will economize the time of their scientists. High-speed transportation, broad band-width communication, special health maintenance, and unlimited bureaucratic assistance are all explained as requirements to get the most out of the most highly capitalized people.

A society with very large tools must rely on multiple devices to keep the majority from claiming the most expensive packages of privilege. These must be reserved for the most productive individuals. The most prestigious way to measure a person's productivity is by the price tag on his education consumption. The higher a person's knowledge capital, the greater the social value placed on the decisions he "makes" and the more legitimate is his claim to high-level packages of industrial outputs.

When the legitimacy of educational certification breaks

down, other more primitive forms of discrimination are bound to assume renewed importance. People are judged to be less valuable manpower because they are born in the third world, because they are black, because they are women, because they belong to the wrong group or party, or because they cannot pass the right battery of tests. The scene is set for the multiplication of minority movements, each one claiming its share, and each one destined to be foiled by its own intent.

Hierarchies must rise and conglomerate as they extend over fewer and larger corporations. A seat in a high-rise job is the most coveted and contested product of expanding industry. The lack of schooling, compounded with sex, color, and peculiar persuasions, now keeps most people down. Minorities organized by women, or blacks, or the unorthodox succeed at best in getting some of their members through school and into an expensive job. They claim victory when they get equal pay for equal rank. Paradoxically, these movements strengthen the idea that unequal graded work is necessary and that high-rise hierarchies are necessary to produce what an egalitarian society needs. If properly schooled, the black porter will blame himself for not being a black lawyer. At the same time, schooling generates a new intensity of frustration which ultimately can act as social dynamite.

It does not matter for what specific purpose minorities now organize if they seek an equal share in consumption, an equal place on the pyramid of production, or equal nominal power in the government of ungovernable tools. As long as a minority acts to increase its share within a growth-oriented society, the final result will be a keener sense of inferiority for most of its members.

Movements that seek control over existing institutions give them a new legitimacy, and also render their contradictions more acute. Changes in management are not revolutions. The shared control of workers and women, or blacks and the young, does not constitute a social reconstruction if what they claim to control are industrial corporations.

Such changes are at best new ways to administer an industrial mode of production which, thanks to these shifts, con-
tinues unchallenged. More commonly, these changes are
professional insurgencies against the *status quo.* They
expand management, and, at an even faster rate, they degrade labor. A new desk usually means more capital-intensive production in one firm and a new guarantee of so-
called underemployment somewhere else in society. A majority loses further productive ability, and a minority is
forced to seek new reasons and weapons to protect its privilege.

New classes of underconsumers and of underemployed
are one of the inevitable by-products of industrial progress.
Organization makes them aware of their common plight.
At present articulate minorities—often claiming the leadership of majorities—seek equal treatment. If one day they
were to seek equal work rather than equal pay—equal inputs rather than equal outputs—they could be the pivot of
social reconstruction. Industrial society could not possibly
resist a strong women's movement, for example, which would
lead to the demand that all people, without distinction, do
equal work. Women are integrated into all classes and
races. Most of their daily activities are perfomed in nonindustrial ways. Industrial societies remain viable precisely
because women are there to perform those daily tasks which
resist industrialization. It is easier to imagine that the North
American continent would cease to exploit the underin-
dustrialization of South America than that it would cease
to use its women for industry-resistant chores. In a society
ruled by the standards of industrial efficiency, housework
is rendered inhuman and devalued. It would be rendered
even less tolerable if it were given *proforma* industrial
status. The further expansion of industry would be brought
to a halt if women forced upon us the recognition that society is no longer viable if a single mode of production prevails. The effective recognition that not two but several
equally valuable, dignified, and important modes of production must coexist within any viable society would bring

industrial expansion under control. Growth would stop if women obtained equally creative work for all, instead of demanding equal rights over the gigantic and expanding tools now appropriated by men.

5. Obsolescence

Convivial reconstruction demands the disruption of the present monopoly of industry, but not the abolition of all industrial production. It does imply the adoption of labor-intensive tools, but not the regression to inefficient tools. It requires a considerable reduction of all kinds of now compulsory therapy, but not the elimination of teaching, guidance, or healing for which individuals take personal responsibility. Neither must a convivial society be stagnant. Its dynamics depend on wide distribution of the power to make effective change. In the present scheme of large-scale obsolescence a few corporate centers of decision making impose compulsory innovation on the entire society. Continued convivial reconstruction depends on the degree to which society protects the power of individuals and of communities to choose their own styles of life through effective, small-scale renewal.

I have shown that social polarization is the result of two complementary factors: the excessive cost of industrially produced and advertised products, and the excessive rarity of jobs that are considered highly productive. Obsolescence, on the other hand, produces devaluation—which is the result not of a certain general rate of change but of change in those products which exercise a radical monopoly. Social polarization depends on the fact that industrial inputs and outputs come in units so large that most people are excluded from them. Obsolescence, on the other hand, can become intolerable even when people are not directly priced out of the market. Product elaboration and obsolescence are two distinct dimensions of overefficiency, both of which underpin a society of hierarchically layered privilege.

It does not really matter if forced obsolescence becomes

destructive of old models or of old functions, if Ford discontinues the distribution of spare parts for its 1955 model, or if the police rule old cars off the road because they lack features that safety lobbyists have made standard. Renewal is intrinsic to the industrial mode of production coupled to the ideology of progress. Products cannot be improved unless huge machines are *retooled*—and in the technical sense engineers have given this word. To make this pay, huge markets must be created for the new model. The most effective way to open a market is to identify the use of what is new as an important privilege. If this identification succeeds, the old model is devalued and the self-interest of the consumer is wedded to the ideology of never-ending and progressive consumption. Individuals are socially graded according to the number of years their bill of goods is out of date. Some people can afford to keep up with the Joneses who buy the latest model, while others still use cars, stoves, and radios that are five to ten years old—and probably spend their vacations in places that are just as many years out of style. They know where they fit on the social ladder.

The social grading of individuals by the age of the things they use is not just a capitalist practice. Wherever the economy is built around the large-scale production of elaborate and obsolescent packages of staples, it is only the privileged who have access to the newest model of services and goods. Only a few nurses get the most recent course in anesthesiological nursing, and only a few functionaries get the new model of a "people's car." The members of this minority within a minority recognize each other by the recent date at which the products they use came onto the market, and it makes little difference whether they use them at home or at work.

Industrial innovations are costly, and managers must justify their high cost by producing measurable proof of their superiority. Under the rule of industrial socialism, pseudoscience will have to provide the alibi, while in market economies, appeal can be made to a survey of consumer opinion. In any case, periodic innovations in goods or tools foster the belief that anything new will be proven better. This belief has become an integral part of the modern world view. It is forgotten that whenever a society lives by this delusion, each marketed unit generates more wants than it satisfies. If new things are made because they are better, then the things most people use are not quite good. New models constantly renovate poverty. The consumer feels the lag between what he has and what he ought to get. He believes that products can be made measurably more valuable and allows himself to be constantly re-educated for their consumption. The "better" replaces the "good" as the fundamental normative concept.

In a society caught up in the race for the better, limits on change are experienced as a threat. The commitment to the better at any cost makes the good impossible at all costs. Failure to renew the bill of goods frustrates the expectation of what is possible, while renewal of the bill of goods intensifies the expectations of unattainable progress. What people have and what they are about to get are equally exasperating to them. Accelerating change has become both addictive and intolerable. At this point the balance among stability, change, and tradition has been upset; society has lost both its roots in shared memories and its bearings for innovation. Judgment on precedents has lost its value.

One of the major objections against a stationary-state economy is the fear that the production of a limited and durable number of goods would set intolerable limits on the freedom of innovation and of scientific exploration. This would be justified if I were discussing the transition from the present industrial society to its next model: clean and limited production of goods and unlimited growth in the service sector. I am not, however, discussing the evolution of industrial society, but the transition to a new mixed mode of production.

Industrial innovations are planned, trivial, and conservative. The renewal of convivial tools would be as unpredictable, creative, and lively as the people who use them. Scientific progress is also dulled by the present identification of research with industrial development. Most of the cost of research derives from its competitive nature and pressure; most of its tools are restricted to people who have been carefully programmed to look at the world through the prisms of profit and power; most of its goals are set by the need for more power and efficiency. Leisurely scientific research does not exclude a bevatron or some ultracentrifuges; removal of access restrictions now created by schools would again admit the curious, rather than the orthodox, to the alchemist's vault; and study for its own sake would produce more surprises than team research on how to eliminate production snags.

A changeless society would be as intolerable for people as the present society of constant change. Convivial reconstruction requires limits on the rate of compulsory change. An unlimited rate of change makes lawful community meaningless. Law is based on the retrospective judgment of peers about circumstances that occur ordinarily and are likely to occur again. If the rate of change which affects all circumstances accelerates beyond some point, such judgments cease to be valid. Lawful society breaks down. Social control does not accommodate community participation and becomes the function of experts. Educators define how people are to be trained and retrained throughout their lives—shaped and reshaped until they fit the demands of industry and are attracted by its profits. Idealogues define what is right or wrong. The tooling of man for the milieu becomes the major industry when this milieu changes beyond a certain rate; then man's need for language and law, for memories and myths, imposes limits to the change of tools.

6. Frustration

I have identified five realms in each of which the efficiency of tools can upset the balance of life. Faulty technology can render the environment uninhabitable. Radical monopoly can force the demand for affluence to the point of paralyzing the ability to work. Overprogramming can transform the world into a treatment ward in which people are constantly taught, socialized, normalized, tested, and reformed. Centralization and packaging of institutionally produced values can polarize society into irreversible structural despotism. And, finally, engineered obsolescence can break all bridges to a normative past. In each or several of these dimensions a tool can threaten survival by making it unfeasible for most people to relate themselves in action to one of the great dimensions of their environment.

In the assessment of society it is not sufficient to select just one of these realms. Each one of these balances must be preserved. Even clean and equally distributed electricity could lead to intolerable radical monopoly of power tools over man's personal energy. Not only compulsory schools but pervasive teaching media can be used to upset the balance of learning or to polarize society into an oppressive meritocracy. Any form of engineering can lead to unendurable obsolescence. It is true that man's physical niche is threatened; but just as he evolved within one particular physiological environment, so he also evolved within a social, political and psychological environment which can also be irreversibly destroyed. Mankind may wither and disappear because he is deprived of basic structures of language, law, and myth, just as much as he can be smothered by smog. Future shock can destroy what is human just as much as radical monopoly or social polarization.

I have argued that in each of five realms conceptual criteria can be used to recognize escalating imbalance. These criteria serve as guidelines for political processes by which the members of a technological society can develop constitutive boundaries within which tools must be kept. Such boundaries circumscribe the kind of power structures that can be kept under the control of people. By growing beyond this range, tools escape political control. Man's ability to claim his rights is extinguished by his bondage to processes over which he has no say. Biological functions, work, meaning, freedom, and roots—insofar as he can still enjoy

them—are reduced to concessions, which optimize the logic
of tools. Man is reduced to an indefinitely malleable resource
of a corporate state. Without constitutive limits translated
into constitutional provisions survival in dignity and freedom is squelched.

Present research is overwhelmingly concentrated in two
directions: research and development for breakthroughs to
the better production of better wares and general systems
analysis concerned with protecting man for further consumption. Future research ought to lead in the opposite di-
rection; let us call it counterfoil research. Counterfoil research also has two major tasks: to provide guidelines for
detecting the incipient stages of murderous logic in a tool;
and to devise tools and tool systems that optimize the balance of life, thereby maximizing liberty for all.

Counterfoil research is not a new branch of science, nor
is it some interdisciplinary project. It is the dimensional
analysis of the relationship of man to his tools. It seems obvious that each person lives in several concentric social environments. To each social environment there corresponds
a set of natural scales. This is true for the primary group, for
the production unit, for the city, the state, and the organization of men on the globe. To each of these social environments there correspond certain characteristic distances, periods, populations, energy sources, and energy sinks. In each
of these dimensions tools that require time periods or spaces
or energies much beyond the order of corresponding natural
scales are dysfunctional. They upset the homeostasis which
renders the particular environment viable. At present we
tend to define human needs in terms of abstract goals and
treat these as problems to which technocrats can apply escalating solutions. What we need is rational research on the
dimensions within which technology can be used by concrete communities to implement their aspirations without
frustrating equivalent aspirations by others.

The barriers beyond which destruction looms are of a different nature from the boundaries within which a society
freely constrains its tools. The former establish the realm of

possible survival; the latter determine the shape of a culturally preferred environment. The former define the conditions for uniform regimentation; the latter set the conditions
of convivial justice. The boundaries of doom are constitutive requirements common to all postindustrial societies. Statutory characteristics setting more narrow bounds
than those absolutely necessary are the result of joint options made in a commonweal, as a result of its members'
defining their life style and their level of liberty.

Supersonic transports could be easily ruled out to protect
the environment, air transport to avoid social polarization,
cars to protect against radical monopoly. The balance of
purpose I want to highlight at this point provides a further
criterion by which to select desirable tools. In view of this
balance it might even be possible to exclude public transportation moving at high velocity.

There is a form of malfunction in which growth does not
yet tend toward the destruction of life, yet renders a tool
antagonistic to its specific aims. Tools, in other words, have
an optimal, a tolerable, and a negative range. Tolerable
overefficiency also disturbs a balance, but a balance of a sub-
tler and more subjective kind than those discussed before.
The balance here threatened is that between personal cost
and return. It can be expressed more generally as the perception of the balance between means and ends. When ends
become subservient to the tools chosen for their sake, the
user first feels frustration and finally either abstains from
their use or goes mad. Compulsory maddening behavior in
Hades was considered the ultimate punishment reserved for
blasphemy. Sisyphus was forced to keep rolling a stone up-
hill, only to see it roll back down. When maddening behavior becomes the standard of a society, people learn to compete for the right to engage in it. Envy blinds people and
makes them compete for addiction.

Wherever the maximum velocity of any one type of commuter vehicle grows beyond a certain mph, the travel time
and the cost of transportation for the median commuter is
increased. If the maximum velocity at any one point of a

commuter system goes beyond a certain mph, most people are obliged to spend more time in traffic jams, or waiting for connections, or recovering from accidents. They will also have to spend more time paying for the transportation system they are compelled to use.

The critical velocity depends to a certain extent on a variety of factors: geography, culture, market controls, level of technology, and money flow. With so many variables affecting a quantity, it would seem that its value could fluctuate over a very wide range. Just the contrary is true. Once it is understood that we refer to any vehicular velocity in the transportation of people within a community, we find that the range within which the critical velocity can vary is very narrow. It is, in fact, so narrow and so low that it seems improbable and not worth the time of most traffic engineers to worry about.

Commuter transportation leads to negative returns when it admits, anywhere in the system, speeds much above those reached on a bicycle. Once the barrier of bicycle velocity is broken at any point in the system, the total per capita monthly time spent at the service of the travel industry increases.

High output leads to time lack. Time becomes scarce, partly because it takes time to consume goods and to undergo therapies, and partly because dependence on production makes abstention from it more costly. The richer we get in a consumer society, the more acutely we become aware of how many grades of value—of both leisure and labor—we have climbed. The higher we are on the pyramid, the less likely we are to give up time to simple idleness and to apparently nonproductive pursuits. The joy of listening to the neighborhood finch is easily overshadowed by stereophonic recordings of "Bird Songs of the World," the walk through the park downgraded by preparations for a packaged bird-watching tour into the jungle. It becomes difficult to economize time when all commitments are for the long run. Staffan Linder points out that there is a strong tendency for us to overcommit the future, so that when the future becomes present, we seem to be conscious all the time of having an acute scarcity, simply because we have committed ourselves to about thirty hours a day instead of twenty-four. In addition to the mere fact that time has competitive uses and high marginal utility in an affluent society, this overcommitment creates a sense of pressure and harriedness.

Life in a society where speedy transportation is taken for granted renders time scarce in both of these ways. Activities related to the use of speedy vehicles by *many* people in a society occupy an increasing percentage of the time budget of *most* members of that society, as the speed of the vehicles increases beyond a certain point. Beyond this point the competition of transportation activities with stationary activities becomes fierce, especially competition for the allocation of limited real estate and available energy. This competition seems to grow exponentially with the rise of speed. The time reserved for commuting displaces both work and leisure time. Hence, the speedier vehicles are, the more it becomes important to keep them filled at all times. If they are individual capsules, they tend to become disproportionately costly and scarce. If they are public vehicles, they tend to be large, and run at infrequent intervals or along only a few routes.

As speed increases, the adaptation of life patterns to vehicles becomes more tyrannical. It becomes necessary to make constant corrections and amendments to the allocation of shorter periods. It becomes necessary to make appointments and commitments months or even years ahead. Since some of these commitments, which have been made at great cost, cannot be kept, there is a sense of constant failure which produces a sense of constant tension. Man has only a limited ability to submit to programming. When speed increases beyond a certain point, the transportation system vies with other systems in exhausting human tolerance for social controls.

Machines turn against men at a much lower level of power than would be ruled out by the first five criteria.

But while these criteria identify necessary safeguards for life and liberty, the *balance of purpose* depends on a different kind of value. Conceptual rather than empirical criteria can be set for the constitutional limitation of power. It ought to be relatively easy for a majority to rule what abuse it will take from any minority, or what damage it will not expose its offspring to. The recognition of the most socially desirable power of a tool is of a different nature; it can only be the outcome of political procedure. The value obtained for time wasted on speed transportation is conditioned by the consensus in a community about the level of its freedom as a concrete option of its civilization.

Transportation beyond bicycle speeds demands power inputs from the environment. Velocity translates directly into power, and soon power needs increase exponentially. In the United States, 22 percent of the energy converted drives vehicles, and another 10 percent keeps roads open for them. The amount of energy is comparable to the total energy—except for domestic heating—required for the combined economies of India and China. The energy used up in the United States for the sole purpose of driving vehicles built to accelerate beyond bicycle speed would suffice to add auxiliary motors to about twenty times that many vehicles for people all over the world who want to move at bicycle speeds and do not or cannot push the pedals because they are sick or old, or because they want to transport a heavy load or move over a great distance, or because they just want to relax. Simply on the basis of equal distribution on a world-wide scale, speeds above those attained by bicycles could be ruled out. It is of course mere fantasy to assume an egalitarian consensus sufficiently strong to accept such a proposal. At closer inspection though, many communities will find that the very same speed limit necessary for equal distribution of mobility is also very close to the optimum velocity giving maximum value to community life. At 20 mph constant speed Phileas Fogg could have made his trip around the world in half of eighty days. Simulation studies would be useful for exploring imaginative policies that seek optimal liberty with convivial power tools. To whose advantage would Calcutta's traffic flow stabilize if speeds were limited to 10 mph? What price would Peru's military pay for limiting the nation's speed to 20 mph? What gains in equality, activity, health, and freedom would result from limiting all other vehicles to the speed of bicycles and sailing ships?

Negative returns are not unique to transportation. Ninety percent of all medical care for patients with terminal diseases is unrelated to their health; such treatment tends to increase suffering and disability without demonstrably lengthening life. The maximum feasibility of service for the optimum care of an individual patient lies within a certain range. Beyond this range medical bills measure the health of a patient in the same way that GNP measures the wealth of a nation. Both add on the same scale the market value of benefits and the defensive expenditures which become necessary to offset the unwanted side effects of their production. The technological escalation of medicine first ceases to serve healing and then ceases to prolong life. It turns into a death-denying ritual of terminal care: a final race in which the personality best fitted to machines turns in the most spectacular performance.

Counterfoil research is concerned first with an analysis of increasing marginal disutility and the menace of growth. It is then concerned with the discovery of general systems of institutional structure which optimize convivial production. This kind of research meets psychological resistance. Growth has become addictive. Like heroin addiction, the habit distorts basic value judgments. Addicts of any kind are willing to pay increasing amounts for declining satisfactions. They have become tolerant to escalating marginal disutility. They are blind to deeper frustration because they are absorbed in playing for always mounting stakes. Minds accustomed to thinking that transportation ought to provide speedy motion rather than reduction of the time and effort spent moving are boggled by this contrary hypothesis. Man is inherently mobile, and speeds higher than those he can achieve by the use of his limbs must be proven to be of great social value to warrant support by public sacrifice.

Counterfoil research must clarify and dramatize the relationship of people to their tools. It ought to hold constantly before the public the resources that are available and the consequences of their use in various ways. It should impress on people the existence of any trend that threatens one of the major balances on which life depends. Counterfoil research leads to the identification of those classes of people most immediately hurt by such trends and helps people to identify themselves as members of such classes. It points out how a particular freedom can be jeopardized for the members of various groups which have otherwise conflicting interests. Counterfoil research involves the public by showing that the demands for freedom of any group or alliance can be identified with the implicit interest of all.

Withdrawal from growth mania will be painful, but mostly for members of the generation which has to experience the transition and above all for those most disabled by consumption. If their plight could be vividly remembered, it might help the next generation avoid what they know would enslave them.

IV

Recovery

I have discussed five dimensions on which the balance of
life depends. In each I have indicated tendencies that must
be kept in equilibrium to maintain the homeostasis which
constitutes human life. I have argued that the control of
natural forces is functional only if the use of nature does
not make nature useless for man. I have argued that institutions are functional when they promote a delicate balance
between what people can do for themselves and what tools
at the service of anonymous institutions can do for them.
Formal instruction also depends on a balance. Special arrangements must never outweigh opportunities for independent learning. An increase in social mobility can render
society more human, but only if at the same time there is
a narrowing of the difference in power which separates
the few from the many. Finally, an increase in the rate of
innovation is of value only when with it rootedness in tradition, fullness of meaning, and security are also strength-
ened.

A tool can grow out of man's control, first to become his
master and finally to become his executioner. Tools can
rule men sooner than they expect: the plow makes man the
lord of a garden but also the refugee from a dust bowl. Nature's revenge can produce children less fit for life than
their fathers, and born into a world less fit for them. *Homo
faber* can be turned into a sorcerer's apprentice. Specialization can make his every day so complicated that it becomes
estranged from his activity. Addiction to progress can enslave all men to a race in which none ever reaches the goal.
There are two ranges in the growth of tools: the range

within which machines are used to extend human capability and the range in which they are used to contract, eliminate, or replace human functions. In the first, man as an individual can exercise authority on his own behalf and therefore assume responsibility. In the second, the machine takes over —first reducing the range of choice and motivation in both the operator and the client, and second imposing its own logic and demand on both. Survival depends on establishing procedures which permit ordinary people to recognize these ranges and to opt for survival in freedom, to evaluate the structure built into tools and institutions so they can exclude those which by their structure are destructive, and control those which are useful. Exclusion of the malignant tool and control of the expedient tool are the two major priorities for politics today. Multiple limits to overefficiency must be expressed in language that is simple and politically effective. This urgent task is faced, however, with three formidable obstacles: the idolatry of science, the corruption of ordinary language, and loss of respect for the formal process by which social decisions are made.

1. *The Demythologization of Science*

Above all, political discussion is stunned by a delusion about science. This term has come to mean an institutional enterprise rather than a personal activity, the solving of puzzles rather than the unpredictably creative activity of individual people. Science is now used to label a spectral production agency which turns out better knowledge just as medicine produces better health. The damage done by this misunderstanding about the nature of knowledge is even more fundamental than the damage done to the conceptions of health, education, or mobility by their identification with institutional outputs. False expectations of better health corrupt society, but they do so in only one particular sense. They foster a declining concern with healthful environments, healthy life styles, and competence in the personal care of one's neighbor. Deceptions about health are circumstantial. The institutionalization of knowledge leads to a more general and degrading delusion. It makes people dependent on having their knowledge produced for them. It leads to a paralysis of the moral and political imagination.

This cognitive disorder rests on the illusion that the knowledge of the individual citizen is of less value than the "knowledge" of science. The former is the opinion of individuals. It is merely subjective and is excluded from policies. The latter is "objective"—defined by science and promulgated by expert spokesmen. This objective knowledge is viewed as a commodity which can be refined, constantly improved, accumulated and fed into a process, now called "decision making." This new mythology of governance by the manipulation of knowledge-stock inevitably erodes reliance on government by people.

The world does not contain any information. It is as it is. Information about it is created in the organism through its interaction with the world. To speak about storage of information outside the human body is to fall into a semantic trap. Books or computers are part of the world. They can yield information when they are looked upon. We move the problem of learning and of cognition nicely into the blind spot of our intellectual vision if we confuse vehicles for potential information with information itself. We do the same when we confuse data for potential decision with decision itself.

Overconfidence in "better knowledge" becomes a self-fulfilling prophecy. People first cease to trust their own judgment and then want to be told the truth about what they know. Overconfidence in "better decision making" first hampers people's ability to decide for themselves and then undermines their belief that they can decide.

The growing impotence of people to decide for themselves affects the structure of their expectations. People are transformed from contenders for scarce resources into competitors for abundant promises. Adjudication by ordeal is replaced by recourse to secular rituals. These rituals are organized as frenzied consumption of the offerings of some menu: a curriculum, a therapy, or a court case. The promise that science will provide affluence for all and for each according to his objectively verified merits deprives personal conflict of its creative legitimacy. People who have unlearned how to decide about their own rights on their own evidence become pawns in a world game operated by megamachines. No longer can each person make his or her own contribution to the constant renewal of society. Recourse to better knowledge produced by science not only voids personal decisions of the power to contribute to an ongoing historical and social process, it also destroys the rules of evidence by which experience is traditionally shared. The knowledge consumer depends on getting packaged programs funneled into him. He finds security in the expectation that his neighbor and his boss have seen the same programs and read the same columns. The procedure by which personal certainties are honestly exchanged is eroded by the increasing recourse to exceptionally qualified knowledge produced by a science, profession, or political party. Mothers poison their children on the adman's or the M.D.'s advice. Even in the courtroom and in parliament, scientific hearsay—well hidden under the veil of expert testimony—biases juridical and political decisions. Judges, governments, and voters abdicate their own evidence about the necessity of resolving conflicts in a situation of defined and permanent scarcity and opt for further growth on the basis of data which they admittedly cannot fully understand.

When communities have grown overconfident in science, they leave it to experts to set the upper limits on growth. This mandate rests on a fallacy. Experts can define standards at levels slightly below those at which people complain with too much force. They can keep the public sullen and forestall mutiny. But closed peer groups cannot be entrusted with self-restraint in furthering their expert knowledge. Nor can we expect them to be representative of the common man. Scientific expertise cannot define what people will tolerate. No person can abdicate the right to decide on this for himself. It is, of course, *possible* to experiment on humans. Nazi doctors explored what the organism can endure. They found out how long the average person can survive torture, but this did not tell them anything about what someone can tolerate. These doctors were condemned under a statute signed in Nuremberg two days after Hiroshima and the day before the bomb was dropped on Nagasaki.

What a population will endure remains beyond experiment. We can tell what happens to particular groups of people under extreme circumstances—in prison, on an expedition, or in an experiment. Such precedents cannot serve as measures for the privations which a society will tolerate as a result of tools or rules made for its service. Scientific measurements may suggest that a certain endeavor threatens a major balance of life. Only the informed judgment of a majority of prudent men who act on the much more complex basis of everyday evidence can determine how to limit individual and social goals. Science can clarify the dimensions of man's realm in the universe. Only a political community can dialectically choose the dimensions of the roof under which its members will live.

2. *The Rediscovery of Language*

Between 1830 and 1850 a dozen inventors formulated the law of the conservation of energy. Most of them were engineers, and independently from each other they redefined the floating life force of the universe in terms of work machines could perform. Measurements that could be taken in the laboratory became the scale by which the mysterious cosmic nexus—called *vis viva* for centuries—could henceforth be defined.

During the same period industry successfully competed with other modes of production for the first time. Industrial performance became the scale according to which human effectiveness in the entire economy was now measured. Housework, farming, handicraft, and subsistence activities ranging from the making of preserves to the self-building of a home began to be viewed as subsidiary or second-rate forms of production. The industrial mode first degraded and later paralyzed the nexus of productive relationships which coexisted in society.

This monopoly of one mode of production over all social relations is much more profound than the competition of firms which overshadows it. In the surface competition the winner is easily recognized as the more capital-intensive factory, the better-organized business, the more exploitative and better-protected branch of industry, the corporation that sheds diseconomies the most unobtrusively or produces for war. On a broad scale this race takes the form of a competition among multinational corporations and industrializing nation-states. But this deadly game among giants diverts attention from the ritual service which the game itself renders to the contestants. As the arena of the contest expands, an industrial structure is imposed on world society. The mode of corporate production establishes a radical monopoly not only over resources and tools but also over the imagination and motivational structure of people. Political systems compete to baptize the same expanding industrial structure into opposing creeds, without recognizing that it is beyond their control. The convergence of corporate monopolies on the deep structural level of society can be called the industrialization of man. This trend must be inverted if people are to be free. But the industrial corruption of language itself makes this issue terribly difficult to formulate.

Language reflects the monopoly of the industrial mode of production over perception and motivation. The tongues of industrial nations identify the fruits of creative work and of human labor with the outputs of industry. The materialization of consciousness is reflected in Western languages. Schools operate by the slogan "education!" while ordinary language asks what children "learn." The functional shift from verb to noun highlights the corresponding impoverishment of the social imagination. People who speak a nominalist language habitually express proprietary relationships to *work* which they *have*. All over Latin America only the salaried employees, whether workers or bureaucrats, say that they *have* work; peasants say that they *do* it: "*Van a trabajar, pero no tienen trabajo.*" Those who have been modernized and unionized expect industries to produce not only more goods but also more work for more people. Not only what men do but also what men want is designated by a noun. "Housing" designates a commodity rather than an activity. People acquire knowledge, mobility, even sensitivity or health. They *have* not only work or fun but even sex.

This shift from verb to noun reflects a transformation in the idea of ownership. "Possessing," "holding," and "seizing" no longer describe the relationships people can have to corporations, such as systems of schools or highways. Possessive statements made about tools come to mean the ability to command their outputs, interest from capital, or merchandise, or some kind of prestige connected with their operation. Fully industrialized man calls his own principally what has been made for him. He says "my education," "my transportation," "my entertainment," "my health" about the commodities he gets from school, car, show business, or doctor. Western languages, and above all English, become almost inseparable from industrial production. Western men might have to learn from other languages that ownership relations can be restructured in a convivial way. For instance, in Micronesian tongues there exist entirely distinct devices to express the relationship I have to my acts (which can no longer be separated from me), to my nose (which can be cut off), to my relatives (who were inflicted on me), to my canoe (without which I could not be a full man), to a drink (which I serve you), or to the same drink (which I intend to swallow).

In a society whose language has undergone this shift, predicates come to be stated in terms of a commodity and claims in terms of competition for a scarce resource. "I want to learn" is translated into "I want to get an education." The decision to do something is turned into the demand for a stake in the gamble of schooling. "I want to walk" is restated as "I need transportation." The subject in the first case designates himself as an actor, and in the second as a consumer. Linguistic change supports the expansion of the industrial arena: competition for institutionalized values is reflected in the use of nominal language. This competition for shares inevitably takes the form of a game. People gamble for what they perceive as nouns. Of course, that competition can be organized either as a zero-sum game, in which one wins when another loses, or as a non-zero-sum game, in which both competitors get more than if either had lost. Compulsory school could be construed as an example of a zero-sum game: there are only winners and losers; by definition school bestows privilege on fewer people than it degrades. An example of the second would be the transition from private to public transport: at least for the time being, more commuters could get faster wherever they want to go.

Conflict does not have to be a competition for scarce commodities. It could also manifest disagreement about which conditions would best remove restraints on autonomous action. Conflict can lead to the creation of new freedom; but this possibility has been obscured by nominalist language. It can create for both parties the right to do, and to do things which by definition are neither commodities nor scarce. Conflict which leads to the right to walk, to participate in shaping society, to speak and communicate equally, to live in clean air or to use convivial tools deprives both adversaries of some affluence for the sake of an incommensurable gain—new liberty.

In some societies the corruption of language has crippled the political fantasy to the point where the difference between a claim to commodities and a right to convivial tools cannot be understood. Limits on tools cannot be publicly discussed. Public blindness to urgent issues is not a new phenomenon. People for decades refused to open their eyes to the urgency of population control, for example. Limiting tools for the sake of freedom and conviviality is now such an issue that cannot be raised. A limit on vehicular velocity as a major election issue seems an implausible idea to the rich and an irrelevant idea to the poor. People who are born next to highways cannot imagine a world without speed, and the peasant in the Andes cannot grasp why anyone should travel that fast. A slowdown as the condition for good transportation sounds shocking. To recommend limits on tools sounds as deeply obscene today as the recommendation for greater sexual frankness and freedom as a condition for a good marriage law would have sounded a generation ago.

The operating code of industrial tools encroaches on everyday language and reduces the poetic self-affirmation of men to a barely tolerated and marginal protest. The consequent industrialization of man can be inverted only if the convivial function of language is recuperated, but with a new level of consciousness. Language which is used by a people jointly claiming and asserting each person's right to share in the shaping of the community becomes, so to speak, a second-order tool to clarify the relationships of a people to engineered instrumentalities.

3. The Recovery of Legal Procedure

Support of an ever-expanding productive society has become the overwhelmingly dominant purpose of the existing structure of politics and law. The procedure by which people decide what ought to be done has become subservient to the ideology that corporations ought to produce more: more knowledge and decisions, more goods and services. This perversion constitutes the third obstacle to the translation of the need for a bounded society into actual social process.

Political parties, legislatures, and the juridical system have been consistently used to foster and protect the growth of schools, unions, hospitals, and road systems, not to speak of industries. Gradually, not only the police but even the courts and the legal system itself have come to be thought of as tools made for the service of an industrial state. That they sometimes protect individuals against industrial claims has become an alibi for their habitual service of legitimizing the further concentration of power. Along with the idolatry of scientific method and the corruption of language, this progressive loss of confidence in political and legal processes is a major obstacle to retooling society.

People come to understand that an alternative society is possible by using clear language. They can bring it about by recovering consciousness of the deep structure by which, in their society, decisions are made. Such a structure exists wherever people form a community. Contradictory decisions can be the outcome of the same process because the structure can be used to define personal values and also to shore up institutional behavior. But the existence of such conflicting results does not contradict the existence of a consistent structure which generates them. People can decide to *get* an education in school even though they have decided that it would be better to learn something on their own. They can let themselves be taken to a hospital, though they have decided to die at home. Just as cognitive dissonance is a foundation for dialectics, so the simultaneous acceptance of contradictory norms proves the existence of normative procedures.

Public confidence in the existence of shared procedures has been shaken because these procedures are constantly misused. They have become tools to support unlimited production through converging arguments that alternately take a moral, a political, or a legal character. Christian churches preach meekness, charity, and austerity but finance industrial programs; socialists enforce a Stalinist mode of production, and the common law has come to favor the firm over the individual. Soon the computer will be used to define at every juncture what should be done for the growth of tools, unless people rediscover that they share a deep commitment to formal procedures by which they can decide how their present major institutions ought to be turned around.

Unless people agree on a process that can be continuously, convivially, and effectively used to control society's tools, the inversion of the present institutional structure cannot be either enacted or, what is more important, precariously maintained. Managers will always re-emerge to increase institutional productivity and capture public support for the better service they promise.

Three objections are usually made whenever law is proposed as a tool for the inversion of society. One of them is rather superficial: not everybody can be a lawyer, and so not everybody can operate the law on his own. This, of course, is true only to some degree. Parajuridical systems could be set up in particular communities and incorporated into the over-all structure. Much wider scope could be given to alternative mechanisms to allow for greater participation by the nonprofessional, such as mediation, conciliation, and arbitration. But insofar as this objection is valid, it is also irrelevant to my point. The law, as it deals with the regulation of large-scale production agencies, can surely be decentralized, demystified and debureaucratized. But even then some social concerns are, and could for a long time remain, complex and of vast range, demanding corresponding legal tools. Precisely if it is to be used for the negotiating of world-wide proscriptions among large communities, each with its own centuries-old traditions, the law as the process enabling us to regulate these concerns is and will remain a tool requiring some experts to operate it. But this does not mean that such experts have to be graduates of a law school, or that they must be members of a closed profession.

The second objection is completely relevant and much more profound: persons who now operate the law as a social tool are deeply infected with the myths that pervade a growth society. Their imagination of the possible and of the feasible is determined by the lore of industry. It would be folly to expect the present corporations of social engineers

of a utilitarian society to turn into the guardians of a convivial one. The critical importance of this observation is
complemented and underlined by a third objection. The
juristic system is not simply a set of written laws; it is a continuing process by which those laws are made and then applied to actual situations. The law is used to impose a given
mind-set on all participants. The resulting content of the
law embodies the ideologies of lawmakers and judges. How
they experience the ideology inherent in a culture becomes
established mythology in the laws they make and apply. The
body of laws that regulates an industrial society inevitably
reflects and reinforces its ideology, social character, and
class structure. "More" is always in the common good—more
power to firms, professions, and parties.

While this objection does indicate a fundamental difficulty against the use of law in an inversion of society, it also
misses the point. I carefully distinguish between a body of
laws and the purely formal structure by which it is made,
just as I have distinguished the use of slogans by which our
institutions operate from the use of ordinary language, and
as I will later distinguish between policies and formal political process. It is the latter and not the former which are
the second order of tools we need, can share, and have to
use.

It is almost impossible to insist strongly enough on the
distinction between means and ends in an epoch in which
purposes have been reduced to operations, in an epoch in
which people "raise" consciousness, movements pretend to
provide "liberation," languages rather than persons are
said to "speak," and politicians "make" revolutions. The
law can again serve to highlight the general difference between substance and what might be called not "due process"
but rather "due procedure."

Two major complementary features of the common law
make its formal structure particularly applicable to the
needs which arise in a profound crisis. One is the inherent
continuity of the system, and the other is its adversary nature. Analogous features can be found in other law systems;

I here choose the Anglo-American system of law as an illustration of my more general point.

The continuity built into the lawmaking process does in one sense conserve the substance of a body of laws. This is less obvious in the legislative stage. Legislators are free to innovate at their own discretion, as long as they stay within a constitutional framework. But they do also have to fit any new law into the context of existing legislation, and this tends to ensure that new legislation will not vary too widely from the over-all tradition of existing law.

The function of the courts in providing continuity to the substance of the law is more obvious. A court applies existing law to actual situations. Like cases are decided alike, or the facts are found to be of a different significance today. The law represents the sovereign authority of the past over the present controversy, the continuity of a dialectic process. The court recognizes the controversy as a social concern and incorporates its resolutions into the body of the law. In the process the social experience of the past is readapted to present needs. The present decision will in turn serve as reference in future cases.

The continuity of the formal structure used in this process is of a different order from the continuous embodiment of one set of prejudices in a set of laws. Considered in this formal sense, the system of continuity is not designed to preserve the content of any existing set of laws. It could even be used to preserve the continuous development of a set of laws that fit an inverted society. There is nothing in most constitutions that prevents the passage of laws setting upper limits to productivity, privilege, professional monopoly, or efficiency. In principle, the existing process of legislatures and courts can, with a reversal of its focus, make and apply such law.

The adversary nature of the common law is equally important. The common law is not formally concerned with what is ethically or technically good. It is a tool for the understanding of mutualities that surface as actual conflicts. It leaves to those directly concerned with a social interest the task of insisting on the protection of their rights or the pursuit of their claims to what they consider to be good. This works in both legislation and jurisprudence; the decision is an act of balancing conflicting interests in a way that is theoretically best for all.

It is obvious that during the last few generations this balance has been wholly distorted in favor of a production-oriented society. But the current misuse of the juristic structure is not a valid argument against its use for precisely the opposite purpose. Interests wholly opposed to such a society, free from the illusion that growth can overcome injustice, and concerned with limits, can in principle use the same tool. It is not, of course, sufficient that new types of plaintiffs appear; it is equally true that the growth illusions of legislators must fade, and that parties must be brought forward to represent their interest in a reassessment of what are now taken as facts.

Not only the legislative but also the juridical process depends on the presentation of conflicting social interests by interested parties for settlement by disinterested tribunals. These tribunals operate in a continuous way. Ideally, judges are ordinary, prudent men or women indifferent to the substance of the issue they are expected to reconcile, and experts in the application of process. In practice, however, tribunals have also come to serve the concentration of power and the increase of industrial production. Not only do judges, like legislators, perceive that a conflict is best balanced when the balance is tipped in favor of the over-all interest of corporations, but society has also conditioned the plaintiffs always to demand more. A larger share of institutional output constitutes the substance of a claim much more frequently than protection against an institution which limits a person's freedom to do something on his own. But this abuse of the formal structure of common law does not corrupt the structure itself.

An objection is frequently raised when adversary procedures are presented as a major tool to oppose industrial growth. Society already heavily relies on such proceedings.

Their extension to new areas is continually recommended. Legal reformers tend to provide new weapons to all classes of disadvantaged: blacks, Indians, women, employees, cripples. As a result proceedings have become cumbersome, costly, and only a few of the interested parties can come forward. Decisions are often delayed until they have lost their relevance. Role-playing is encouraged, and this often creates new tensions between artificial groups. In going out of the way to create structures so that adversary processes may be used, decisions are made scarce.

This objection is very relevant if it opposes the proliferation of adversary proceedings in the resolution of conflicts between people. But neither the conflict between individuals nor the competition between groups is the substance of our issue. The fundamental conflict in society is about acts, facts, and things on which people are opposed to corporations. Formal adversary procedure is the paradigmatic tool for citizens to oppose the threat of industry to their basic liberties. This is the process suited to the opposition of two partners whom the law has rendered equal, in which the aggrieved party is interested in disputing one fact or a relevant law or principle, and considers this issue the only continuing interest he has in common with the other. A group of citizens interested in retooling society is not concerned with negotiations or mediation but with direct opposition to the industrial mode of production and its undue expansion in a specific instance.

Like ordinary English, formal process is a convivial tool. Undoubtedly, industrial institutions have entrenched themselves by corrupting the habitual use of these tools by individuals and communities. Yet language and formal process remain intrinsically distinct from the purposes for which they are used. People can defend language and legal procedure as inherently theirs; they can find in their inalienable natures the confidence to use their unchanged formal structures to express contents entirely opposed to those for which they were taught to use them in their childhood. The formal structure of law still offers a process by which the

ordinary citizen can present to society his own practical interest in conflict with the interest of a corporation, even
when this corporation is an agency of the state, and even if
this interest favors or opposes any functioning or proposed
program.

It would be absurd to expect that professionals who are
experts in the corrupt use of language or of law could suddenly think clearly and proceed rightly. Educators who are
aware of the breakdown of schools usually engage in a frantic search for advice that permits them to teach more people
about more things. Doctors tend to believe that at least some
of the generally useful knowledge they hold cannot be expressed outside their hieratic code. It is useless to expect the
American Medical Association, the National Education
Association, or the association of traffic engineers to explain
in ordinary language the professional gangsterism of their
colleagues. It would be equally fruitless to count on present
legislators, lawyers, and judges to recognize the independence of what is right from the preconceived good, which
for them is identical with the higher output of goods by
corporations. They are trained to adjust any conflict in
favor of overall industrial growth. But just as an exceptional
doctor here and there helps people live responsibly, to suffer
as a matter of fact, and to face death, so an exceptional lawyer can help people use the formal structure of the law to
represent their interest in a convivial society. Even though
he will probably be frustrated in his claims, he can use the
courtroom drama to make his point.

Legal procedure applied to a society filled by optimism
about its expanding tools has turned into the most effective
instrument for the social control of people at the service of
these tools. To advance an industrial society, the law is systematically used for social engineering and the continually
more complete and effective elimination of waste and fric-
tion in the megamachine. Anglo-American industry has
consistently been more successful, in the long run, than the
industry of socialist countries. Law is more effective than
centralized planning in bringing and keeping people under

the rule of machines. Yet the current misuse of the juristic structure is not a valid argument against its use for precisely the opposite purpose, though it suggests caution against overly optimistic hopes for such an inverted use.

Most of the present laws and present legislators, most of the present courts and their decisions, most of the claimants and their demands are deeply corrupted by an overarching industrial consensus: that more is better, and that corporations serve the public interest better than men. But this entrenched consensus does not invalidate my thesis that any revolution which neglects the use of formal legal and political procedures will fail. Only an active majority in which all individuals and groups insist for their own reasons on their own rights, and whose members share the same convivial procedure, can recover the rights of men against corporations.

The use of procedure for the purpose of hampering, stopping, and inverting our major institutions will appear to their managers and addicts as a misuse of the law and as subversion of the only order which they recognize. The use of due convivial procedure appears corrupt and criminal to the bureaucrat, even one who calls himself a judge.

V

Political Inversion

If within the very near future man cannot set limits to the interference of his tools with the environment and practice effective birth control, the next generations will experience the gruesome apocalypse predicted by many ecologists. Faced with these impending disasters, society can stand in wait of survival within limits set and enforced by bureaucratic dictatorship. Or it can engage in a political process by the use of legal and political procedures. Ideologically biased interpretations of the past have made the recognition of political process increasingly difficult. Liberty has been interpreted as a right to power tools, a right claimed without reasonable limitation by individuals and private associations in capitalist countries and by the state in socialist societies. Recovery becomes feasible only if the fundamental structure of Western societies is clearly recognized and reclaimed. Analogous efforts to recover entirely different formal structures will become necessary when former political or cultural colonies shake off the Western mode of production.

The bureaucratic management of human survival is unacceptable on both ethical and political grounds. It would also be as futile as former attempts at mass therapy. This does not, of course, mean that a majority might not at first submit to it. People could be so frightened by the increasing evidence of growing population and dwindling resources that they would voluntarily put their destiny into the hands of Big Brothers. Technocratic caretakers could be mandated to set limits on growth in every dimension, and to set them just at the point beyond which further production would mean utter destruction. Such a *kakotopia* could maintain the industrial age at the highest endurable level of output.

Man would live in a plastic bubble that would protect his survival and make it increasingly worthless. Since man's tolerance would become the most serious limitation to growth, the alchemist's endeavor would be renewed in the attempt to produce a monstrous type of man fit to live among reason's dreams. A major function of engineering would become the psychogenetic tooling of man himself as a condition for further growth. People would be confined from birth to death in a world-wide schoolhouse, treated in a world-wide hospital, surrounded by television screens, and the man-made environment would be distinguishable in name only from a world-wide prison.

The alternative to managerial fascism is a political process by which people decide how much of any scarce resource is the most any member of society can claim; a process in which they agree to keep limits relatively stationary over a long time, and by which they set a premium on the constant search for new ways to have an ever larger percentage of the population join in doing ever more with ever less. Such a political choice of a frugal society remains a pious dream unless it can be shown that it is not only necessary but also possible: (1) to define concrete procedures by which more people are enlightened about the nature of our present crisis and will come to understand that limits are necessary and a convivial life style desirable; (2) to bring the largest number of people into now suppressed organizations which claim their right to a frugal life style and keep them satisfied and therefore committed to convivial life; and (3) to discover and revalue the political or legal tools that are accepted within a society and learn how to use them to establish and protect convivial life where it emerges. Such procedures may sound idealistic at the present moment. This is not proof that they cannot become effective as the present crisis deepens.

1. *Myths and Majorities*

The ultimate obstacle to the restructuring of society is not the lack of information about which limits are needed, nor the lack of people who would accept them if they became inevitable, but the power of political myths.

Almost everyone in rich societies is a destructive consumer. Almost everyone is, in some way, engaged in aggression against the milieu. Destructive consumers constitute a numerical majority. Myth transforms them into a political one. Numerical majorities come to form a mythical voting bloc on a nonexistent issue; "they" are invoked as the unbeatable guardians of vested interest in growth. This mythical majority paralyzes political action. At closer inspection, "they" are a number of reasonable individuals. One is an ecologist who takes a jet plane to a conference on protecting the environment from further pollution. Another is an economist who knows that growing efficiency renders work increasingly scarce; he tries to create new sources of employment. Neither of them has the same interests as the slum dweller in Detroit who purchases his color TV on time. The three belong no more to a voting bloc that will defend growth than clerks, repairmen, and salesmen are somehow politically homogenized because each fears for his job, needs a car, and wants medicine for his children.

There can be no such thing as a majority opposed to an issue that has not arisen. A majority agitating for limits to growth is as ludicrous a concept as one demanding growth at all cost. Majorities are not created by shared ideologies. They develop out of enlightened self-interest. The most that even the best of ideologies can do is interpret this interest. The stance each man or woman takes when a social problem becomes an overwhelming threat depends on two factors: the first is how a smoldering conflict erupts into a political issue demanding attention and partisan action; the second is the existence of new elites which can provide an interpretative framework for new—and hitherto unexpected—alignments of interest.

2. *From Breakdown to Chaos*

I can only conjecture on how the breakdown of industrial society will ultimately become a critical issue. But I can make rather firm statements about the qualifications for providing guidance within the coming crisis. I believe that growth will grind to a halt. The total collapse of the industrial monopoly on production will be the result of synergy in the failure of the multiple systems that fed its expansion. This expansion is maintained by the illusion that careful systems engineering can stabilize and harmonize present growth, while in fact it pushes all institutions simultaneously toward their second watershed. Almost overnight people will lose confidence not only in the major institutions but also in the miracle prescriptions of the would-be crisis managers. The ability of present institutions to define values such as education, health, welfare, transportation, or news will suddenly be extinguished because it will be recognized as an illusion.

This crisis may be triggered by an unforeseen event, as the Great Depression was touched off by the Wall Street Crash. Some fortuitous coincidence will render publicly obvious the structural contradictions between stated purposes and effective results in our major institutions. People will suddenly find obvious what is now evident to only a few: that the organization of the entire economy toward the "better" life has become the major enemy of the *good* life. Like other widely shared insights, this one will have the potential of turning public imagination inside out. Large institutions can quite suddenly lose their respectability, their legitimacy, and their reputation for serving the public good. It happened to the Roman Church in the Reformation, to royalty in the Revolution. The unthinkable became obvious overnight: that people could and would behead their rulers.

Sudden change is of a different order than feedback or

evolution. Observe the whirlpools below a waterfall. For many seasons the eddies stay in the same place no matter whether the water is high or low. Then, suddenly, one more stone falls into the basin, the entire array changes, and the old can never be reconstructed. People who invoke the specter of a hopelessly growth-oriented majority seem incapable of envisaging political behavior in a crash. Business ceases to be as usual when the populace loses confidence in industrial productivity, and not just in paper currency.

It is still possible to face the breakdown of each of our various systems in a separate perspective. No remedy seems to work, but we can still find resources to support every remedy proposed. Governments think they can deal with the breakdown of utilities, the disruption of the educational system, intolerable transportation, the chaos of the judicial process, the violent disaffection of the young. Each is dealt with as a separate phenomenon, each is explained by a different report, each calls for a new tax and a new program. Squabbles about alternative remedies give credibility to both: free schools vs. public schools double the demand for education; satellite cities vs. monorails for commuters make the growth of cities seem inexorable; higher professional standards in medicine vs. more paramedical professions further aggrandize the health professions. Since each of the proposed remedies appeals to some, the usual solution is an attempt to try both. The result is a further effort to make the pie grow, and to forget that it is pie in the sky.

The Coolidge approach to the warnings of the Depresson is now applied to the signs of a much more radical crisis. General systems analysis is trusted to relate the institutional breakdowns to each other, which only leads to more planning, centralization, and bureaucracy in order to achieve control over population, affluence, and inefficient industry. Unemployment in the manufacturing sector is supposed to be compensated for by growth in the output of decisions, controls, and therapies. Fascination with industry and mechanical production still blinds people to the possibility of a postindustrial society in which several distinct modes of production would complement each other. Trying to bring about an era which is both hyperindustrial and ecologically feasible, they accelerate the breakdown of several other non-physical and equally fundamental dimensions of the balance of life.

It would be a mere exercise in geomancy to predict which series of events will play the role of the Wall Street Crash as catalyst of the first crisis of, not just in, industrial society. But it would be folly not to expect in the very near future an event whose effects will jam the growth of tools. When this happens, the noise that accompanies the crash will distract attention from seeing it in proper perspective.

We still have a chance to understand the causes of the coming crisis, and to prepare for it. If we are to anticipate its effects, we must investigate how sudden change can bring about the emergence into power of previously submerged social groups. It is not calamity as such that creates these groups; it is much less calamity that brings about their emergence; but calamity weakens the prevailing powers which have excluded the submerged from participation in the social process. It is the power of surprise that weakens control, that shakes up the established controllers, and brings to the top those people who have not lost their bearings.

When controls are weakened, those accustomed to control must seek new allies. In the weakened economic-industrial state of the Great Depression, the establishment could not do without organized labor, so organized labor got its share of power within the structure. In the weakened labor market during the Second World War, industry could not do without black labor. The blacks began to assert their power.

3. Insight into Crisis

Forces tending to limit production are already at work within society. Public, counterfoil research can significantly help these individuals become more cohesive and self-conscious in their indictment of growth they consider destructive. We can anticipate that their voices will acquire new resonance when the crisis of overproductive society becomes acute. They form no constituency, but they are spokesmen for a majority of which everyone is a potential member. The more unexpectedly the crisis comes, the more suddenly their velleities can turn into a program. But the ability to direct events at that moment depends on how well these minorities grasp the profound nature of the crisis, and know how to state it in effective language: to declare what they want, what they can do, and what they do not need. The critical use of ordinary language is the first pivot in a political inversion. A second pivot is needed.

Further growth must lead to a multiple catastrophe. That people would accept multiple limits to growth without catastrophe seems highly improbable. The inevitable catastrophic event could be either a crisis in civilization or its end: end by annihilation or end in B. F. Skinner's world-wide concentration camp run by a T. E. Frazier. The fore-seeable catastrophe will be a true crisis—that is, the occasion for a choice—only if at the moment it strikes the necessary social demands can be effectively expressed. They must be represented by people who can demonstrate that the breakdown of the current industrial illusion is for them a condition for choosing an effective and convivial mode of production. The preparation of such groups is the key task of new politics at the present moment.

I have already argued that these groups must be prepared to provide a logically coherent analysis of the catastrophic event and to communicate it in ordinary language. I have argued that they must be prepared to propose the necessity for a bounded society in practical terms that have general appeal. Sacrifice must be shown as the inevitable price for different groups of people to get what they want—or at least to be liberated from what has become intolerable. But beyond using words to describe the limits as both necessary and appealing, the leadership of these groups must be prepared to use a social tool that is fit to ordain what is good enough for all. It must be a tool which, like language, is respected by all; a tool which, like language, does not lose its power because of the purpose to which it has been put in recent history; a tool which, like language, possesses a fundamental structure that misuse cannot totally corrupt.

I have already argued that such a tool can only be the formal structure of politics and law. At the moment of the crash which is industrial rather than simply financial, the transformation of catastrophe into crisis depends on the confidence an emerging group of clear-thinking and feeling people can inspire in their peers. They must then argue that the transition to a convivial society can be, and must be, the result of conscious use of disciplined procedure that recognizes the legitimacy of conflicting interests, the historical precedent out of which the conflict arose, and the necessity of abiding by the decision of peers. Convivially used procedure guarantees that an institutional revolution will remain a tool whose goals emerge as they are enacted; the conscious use of procedure in a continually antibureaucratic sense is the only possible protection against the revolution itself becoming an institution. Whether the application of this procedure to the inversion of all major institutions of society is then called a cultural revolution, or the recuperation of the formal structure of law, or participatory socialism or a return to the spirit of the *Fueros de España*, is merely a matter of labeling.

4. Sudden Change

When I speak about emerging interest groups and their preparation, I am not speaking of action groups, or of a church, or of new kinds of experts. I am above all not speaking about one political party which could assume power at a moment of crisis. Management of the crisis would make catastrophe irreversible. A well-knit, well-trained party can establish its power at the moment of a crisis in which the choice to be made is one within an over-all system. Such was the Great Depression. What was at issue was control over the tools of production. Such were the events which brought the Marxists to power in Eastern Europe. But the crisis I have described as imminent is not a crisis within industrial society, but a crisis of the industrial mode of production itself. The crisis I have described confronts people with a choice between convivial tools and being crushed by machines. The only response to this crisis is a full recognition of its depth and an acceptance of inevitable self-limitations. The more varied the perspectives from which this insight is shared by interest groups and the more disparate the interests that may be protected only by a reduction of power within society, the greater the probability that the inevitable will be recognized as such.

I am also not speaking about a majority opposed to growth on some abstract principles. Such a majority is unfeasible. A well-organized elite, vocally promulgating an antigrowth orthodoxy, is indeed conceivable. It is probably now forming. But such a programmatic antigrowth elite would be highly undesirable. By pushing people to accept limits to industrial output without questioning the basic industrial structure of modern society, it would inevitably provide more power to the growth-optimizing bureaucrats and become their pawn. One of the first results of transition toward a stable-state industrial economy would be the development of a labor-intensive, highly disciplined, and growing subsector of production that would control people by giving them jobs. Such a stabilized production of highly rationalized and standardized goods and services would be—if this were possible—even further away from convivial production than the industrial-growth society we have now.

The proponents of a bounded society have no need to put together some kind of majority. A voting majority in a democracy is not motivated by the explicit commitment of all its members to some specific ideology or to some particular value. A voting majority in favor of a specific institutional limitation would have to be composed of very disparate elements: those seriously aggrieved by some aspect of overproduction, those who do not profit from it, and those who may have objections to the overall organization of society—but not directly to the specific limit being set. How this functions in times of normal politics can be well illustrated by the example of school. Some people are childless and resent the school tax. Others feel they are taxed more heavily and served less well than their peers in another district. Others object to tax support of schools since they want to send their children to parochial schools. Others object to compulsory schooling as such: some because it does harm to the young and others because it fosters discrimination. All these people could form a voting majority, but not a party or a sect. Under present circumstances they might succeed in cutting school down to size, but thereby they would merely assure its more legitimate survival. A majority vote to limit one major institution tends to be conservative when business is as usual.

But a majority can have the contrary effect in a crisis which affects society on a deeper level. The joint arrival of several institutions at their second watershed is the beginning of such a crisis. The crash that will follow must make it clear that industrial society as such—and not just its separate institutions—has outgrown the range of its effectiveness.

The nation-state has become so powerful that it cannot perform its stated functions. Just as General Vo Nguyen Giap could use the U.S. military machine to win his war, so the multinational corporations and professions can now use the law and the two-party system to establish their empire. But while democracy in the United States can survive a victory by Giap, it cannot survive one by ITT and its like. As a total crisis approaches, it becomes more obvious that the nation-state has grown into the holding corporation for a multiplicity of self-serving tools, and the political party into an instrument to organize stockholders for the occasional election of boards and presidents. In this situation, parties support each voter's right to claim higher levels of *individual* consumption and to enforce thereby higher levels of *industrial* consumption. People can claim cars, but the appropriation of society's over-all resources by a transportation system which determines that cars are useful is left to the decision of experts. Such parties support a state whose only purpose is the support of an increasing GNP, and they are obviously useless at the moment of a general crash.

When business is normal, the procedural opposition between corporations and clients usually heightens the legitimacy of the latter's dependence. But at the moment of a structural crisis not even the voluntary reduction of over-efficiency on the part of major institutions will keep any of them functioning. A general crisis opens the way to social reconstruction. The loss of legitimacy of the state as a holding corporation does not destroy, but reasserts, the need for constitutional procedure. The loss of confidence in parties that have become stockholders' factions brings out the importance of adversary procedures in politics. A loss of credibility of opposing claims for more individual consumption only highlights the importance of the use of adversary procedures when the issue to be decided upon is the reconciliation of opposing sets of society-wide limitations. The same general crisis that could easily lead to one-man rule, expert government, and ideological orthodoxy is also the great opportunity to reconstruct a political process in which all participate.

The structures of political and legal procedures are integral to one another. Both shape and express the structure of freedom in history. If this is recognized, the framework of due procedure can be used as the most dramatic, symbolic, and convivial tool in the political area. The appeal to law remains powerful even where society makes access to legal machinery a privilege, or where it systematically denies justice, or where it cloaks despotism in the mantle of show tribunals. Even when he who upholds the formal structure of ordinary language and procedure earns the scorn, ridicule, and persecution of his fellow revolutionaries, the appeal of an individual to the formal structure embedded in a people's history remains the most powerful instrument to say the truth and denounce the cancerous domination of the industrial dominance over production as the ultimate form of idolatry. I feel almost unbearable anguish when faced by the fact that only the word recovered from history should be left to us as the power for stemming disaster. Yet only the word in its weakness can associate the majority of people in the revolutionary inversion of inevitable violence into convivial reconstruction.

Reconstruction for poor countries means adopting a set of negative design criteria within which their tools are kept, in order to advance directly into a postindustrial era of conviviality. The limits to choose are of the same order as those which hyperindustrialized countries will have to adopt for the sake of survival and at the cost of their vested interest. Such social reconstruction cannot be supported by a high-powered army, both because the maintenance of such an army would foil reconstruction and because no such army would be powerful enough. Defense of conviviality is possible only if undertaken by the people with tools they control. Imperialist mercenaries can poison or maim but never conquer a people who have chosen to set boundaries to their tools for the sake of conviviality.

ABOUT THE AUTHOR

IVAN ILLICH was born in Vienna and grew up in Europe, the United States, and Puerto Rico. In 1964 he helped set up the Center for Intercultural Documentation (CIDOC) in Cuernavaca, Mexico. At CIDOC he directs research seminars on institutional alternatives in a technological society, with special focus on Latin America. Ivan Illich's writings have appeared in *The New York Review of Books, Saturday Review, Esprit, Kursbuch, Siempre, America,* and *Temps Modernes.* He is the author of *Deschooling Society* in the *World Perspectives* series, which is planned and edited by Ruth Nanda Anshen.

WORLD PERSPECTIVES

What This Series Means

It is the thesis of *World Perspectives* that man is in the process of developing a new consciousness which, in spite of his apparent spiritual and moral captivity, can eventually lift the human race above and beyond the fear, ignorance, and isolation which beset it today. It is to this nascent consciousness, to this concept of man born out of a universe perceived through a fresh vision of reality, that *World Perspectives* is dedicated.

My Introduction to this Series is not of course to be construed as a prefatory essay for each individual book. These few pages simply attempt to set forth the general aim and purpose of the Series as a whole. They try to point to the principle of permanence within change and to define the essential nature of man, as presented by those scholars who have been invited to participate in this intellectual and spiritual movement.

Man has entered a new era of evolutionary history, one in which rapid change is a dominant consequence. He is contending with a fundamental change, since he has intervened in the evolutionary process. He must now better appreciate this fact and then develop the wisdom to direct the process toward his fulfillment rather than toward his destruction. As he learns to apply his understanding of the physical world for practical purposes, he is, in reality, extending his innate capacity and augmenting his ability and his need to communicate as well as his ability to think and to create. And as a result, he is substituting a goal-directed evolutionary process in his struggle against environmental hardship for the slow, but effective, biological evolution which produced modern man through mutation and natural selection. By intelligent intervention in the evolutionary process man has greatly accelerated and greatly expanded the range of his possibilities. But he has not changed the basic fact that it remains a trial and error process, with the danger of taking paths that lead to sterility of mind and heart, moral apathy and intellectual inertia; and even producing social dinosaurs unfit to live in an evolving world.

Only those spiritual and intellectual leaders of our epoch who have a paternity in this extension of man's horizons are invited to participate in this Series: those who are aware of the truth that beyond the divisiveness among men there exists a primordial unitive power since we are all bound together by a common humanity more fundamental than any unity of dogma; those who recognize that the centrifugal force which has scattered and atomized mankind must be replaced by an integrating structure and process capable of bestowing meaning and purpose on existence; those who realize that science itself, when not inhibited by the limitations of its own methodology, when chastened and humbled, commits man to an indeterminate range of yet undreamed consequences that may flow from it.

Virtually all of our disciplines have relied on conceptions which are now incompatible with the Cartesian axiom, and with the static world view we once derived from it. For underlying the new ideas, including those of modern physics, is a unifying order, but it is not causality; it is purpose, and not the purpose of the universe and of man, but the purpose *in* the universe and *in* man. In other words, we seem to inhabit a world of dynamic process and structure. Therefore we need a calculus of potentiality rather than one of probability, a dialectic of polarity, one in which unity and diversity are redefined as simultaneous and necessary poles of the same essence.

Our situation is new. No civilization has previously had to face the challenge of scientific specialization, and our response must be new. Thus this Series is committed to ensure that the spiritual and moral needs of man as a human being and the scientific and intellectual resources at his command for *life* may be brought into a productive, meaningful and creative harmony.

In a certain sense we may say that man now has regained his former geocentric position in the universe. For a picture of the Earth has been made available from distant space, from the lunar desert, and the sheer isolation of the Earth has become plain. This is as new and as powerful an idea in history as any that has ever been born in man's consciousness. We are all becoming seriously concerned with our natural environment. And this concern is not only the result of the warnings given by biologists, ecologists and conservationists. Rather it is the result of a deepening awareness that something new has happened, that the planet Earth is a unique and precious place. Indeed, it may not be a mere coincidence that this awareness should have been born at the exact moment when man took his first step into outer space.

This Series endeavors to point to a reality of which scientific theory has revealed only one aspect. It is the commitment to this reality that lends universal intent to a scientist's most original and solitary thought. By acknowledging this frankly we shall restore science to the great family of human aspirations by which men hope to fulfill themselves in the world community as thinking and sentient beings. For our problem is to discover a principle of differentiation and yet relationship lucid enough to justify and to purify scientific, philosophic and all other knowledge, both discursive and intuitive, by accepting their interdependence. This is the crisis in consciousness made articulate through the crisis in science. This is the new awakening.

Each volume presents the thought and belief of its author and points to the way in which religion, philosophy, art, science, economics, politics and history may constitute that form of human activity which takes the fullest and most precise account of variousness, possibility, complexity and difficulty. Thus *World Perspectives* endeavors to define that ecumenical power of the mind and heart which enables man through his mysterious greatness to re-create his life.

This Series is committed to a re-examination of all those sides of human endeavor which the specialist was taught to believe he could safely leave aside. It attempts to show the structural kinship between subject and object; the indwelling of the one in the other. It interprets present and past events impinging on human life in our growing World Age and envisages what man may yet attain when summoned by an unbending inner necessity to the quest of what is most exalted in him. Its purpose is to offer new vistas in terms of world and human development while refusing to betray the intimate correlation between universality and individuality, dynamics and form, freedom and destiny. Each author deals with the increasing realization that spirit and nature are not separate and apart; that intuition and reason must regain their importance as the means of perceiving and fusing inner being with outer reality.

World Perspectives endeavors to show that the conception of wholeness, unity, organism is a higher and more concrete conception than that of matter and energy. Thus an enlarged meaning of life, of biology, not as it is revealed in the test tube of the laboratory but as it is experienced within the organism of life itself, is attempted in this Series. For the principle of life consists in the tension which connects spirit with the realm of matter, symbiotically joined. The element of life is dominant in the very texture of nature, thus rendering life, biology, a transempirical science. The laws of life have their origin beyond their mere physical manifestations and compel us to consider their spiritual source. In fact, the widening of the conceptual framework has not only served to restore order within the respective branches of knowledge, but has also disclosed analogies in man's position regarding the analysis and synthesis of experience in apparently separated domains of knowledge, suggesting the possibility of an ever more embracing objective description of the meaning of life.

Knowledge, it is shown in these books, no longer consists in a manipulation of man and nature as opposite forces, nor in the reduction of data to mere statistical order, but is a means of liberating mankind from the destructive power of fear, pointing the way toward the goal of the rehabilit⸻⸻ of the human will and the rebirth of faith and co⸻⸻⸻ in the human person. The works published also to reveal that the cry for patterns, systems and authorities is growing less insistent as the desire grows stronger in both East and West for the recovery of a dignity, integrity and self-realization which are the inalienable rights of man who may now guide change by means of conscious purpose in the light of rational experience.

The volumes in this Series endeavor to demonstrate that only in a society in which awareness of the problems of science exists, can its discoveries start great waves of change in human culture, and in such a manner that these discoveries may deepen and not erode the sense of universal human community. The differences in the disciplines, their epistemological exclusiveness, the variety of historical experiences, the differences of traditions, of cultures, of languages, of the arts, should be protected and preserved. But the interrelationship and unity of the whole should at the same time be accepted.

The authors of *World Perspectives* are of course aware that the ultimate answers to the hopes and fears which pervade modern society rest on the moral fibre of man, and on the wisdom and responsibility of those who promote the course of its development. But moral decisions cannot dispense with an insight into the interplay of the objective elements which offer and limit the choices made. Therefore an understanding of what the issues are, though not a sufficient condition, is a necessary prerequisite for directing action toward constructive solutions.

Other vital questions explored relate to problems of international understanding as well as to problems dealing with prejudice and the resultant tensions and antagonisms. The growing perception and responsibility of our World Age point to the new reality that the individual person and the collective person supplement and integrate each other; that the thrall of totalitarianism of both left and right has been shaken in the universal desire to recapture the authority of truth and human totality. Mankind can finally place its trust not in a proletarian authoritarianism, not in a secular humanism, both of which have betrayed the spiritual property right of history, but in a sacramental brotherhood and in the unity of knowledge. This new consciousness has created a widening of human horizons beyond every parochialism, and a revolution in human thought comparable to the basic assumption, among the ancient Greeks, of the sovereignty of reason; corresponding to the great effulgence of the moral conscience articulated by the Hebrew prophets; analogous to the fundamental assertions of Christianity; or to the beginning of the new scientific era, the era of the science of dynamics, the experimental foundations of which were laid by Galileo in the Renaissance.

An important effort of this Series is to re-examine the contradictory meanings and applications which are given today to such terms as democracy, freedom, justice, love, peace, brotherhood and God. The purpose of such inquiries is to clear the way for the foundation of a genuine *world* history not in terms of nation or race or culture but in terms of man in relation to God, to himself, his fellow man and the universe, that reach beyond immediate self-interest. For the meaning of the World Age consists in respecting man's hopes and dreams which lead to a deeper understanding of the basic values of all peoples.

World Perspectives is planned to gain insight into the meaning of man, who not only is determined by history but who also determines history. History is to be understood as concerned not only with the life of man on this planet but as including also such cosmic influences as interpenetrate our human world. This generation is discovering that history does not conform to the social optimism of modern civilization and that the organization of human communities and the establishment of freedom and peace are not only intellectual achievements but spiritual and moral achievements as well, demanding a cherishing of the wholeness of human personality, the "unmediated wholeness of feeling and thought," and constituting a never-ending challenge to man, emerging from the abyss of meaninglessness and suffering, to be renewed and replenished in the totality of his life.

Justice itself, which has been "in a state of pilgrimage and crucifixion" and now is being slowly liberated from the grip of social and political demonologies in the East as well as in the West, begins to question its own premises. The modern revolutionary movements which have challenged the sacred institutions of society by protecting social injustice in the name of social justice are here examined and re-evaluated.

In the light of this, we have no choice but to admit that the *un*freedom against which freedom is measured must be retained with it, namely, that the aspect of truth out of which the night view appears to emerge, the darkness of our time, is as little abandonable as is man's subjective advance. Thus the two sources of man's consciousness are inseparable, not as dead but as living and complementary, an aspect of that "principle of complementarity" through which Niels Bohr has sought to unite the quantum and the wave, both of which constitute the very fabric of life's radiant energy.

There is in mankind today a counterforce to the sterility and danger of a quantitative, anonymous mass culture; a new, if sometimes imperceptible, spiritual sense of convergence toward human and world unity on the basis of the sacredness of each human person and respect for the plurality of cultures. There is a growing awareness that equality may not be evaluated in mere numerical terms but is proportionate and analogical in its reality. For when equality is equated with interchangeability, individuality is negated and the human person transmuted into a faceless mask.

We stand at the brink of an age of a world in which human life presses forward to actualize new forms. The false separation of man and nature, of time and space, of freedom and security, is acknowledged, and we are faced with a new vision of man in his organic unity and of history offering a richness and diversity of equality and majesty of scope hitherto unprecedented. In relating the accumulated wisdom of man's spirit to the new reality of the World Age, in articulating its thought and belief, *World Perspectives* seeks to encourage a renaissance of hope in society and of pride in man's decision as to what his destiny will be.

World Perspectives is committed to the recognition that all great changes are preceded by a vigorous intellectual re-evaluation and reorganization. Our authors are aware that the sin of *hubris* may be avoided by showing that the creative process itself is not a free activity if by free we mean arbitrary, or unrelated to cosmic law. For the creative process in the human mind, the developmental process in organic nature and the basic laws of the inorganic realm may be but varied expressions of a universal formative process. Thus *World Perspectives* hopes to show that although the present apocalyptic period is one of exceptional tensions, there is also at work an exceptional movement toward a compensating unity which refuses to violate the ultimate moral power at work in the universe, that very power upon which all human effort must at last depend. In this way we may come to understand that there exists an inherent independence of spiritual and mental growth which, though conditioned by circumstances, is never determined by circumstances. In this way the great plethora of human knowledge may be correlated with an insight into the nature of human nature by being attuned to the wide and deep range of human thought and human experience.

Incoherence is the result of the present disintegrative processes in education. Thus the need for *World Perspectives* expresses itself in the recognition that natural and man-made ecological systems require as much study as isolated particles and elementary reactions. For there is a basic correlation of elements in nature as in man which cannot be separated, which compose each other and alter each other mutually. Thus we hope to widen appropriately our conceptual framework of reference. For our epistemological problem consists in our finding the proper balance between our lack of an all-embracing principle relevant to our way of evaluating life and in our power to express ourselves in a logically consistent manner.

Our Judeo-Christian and Greco-Roman heritage, our Hellenic tradition, has compelled us to think in exclusive categories. But our *experience* challenges us to recognize a

totality richer and far more complex than the average ob-
server could have suspected—a totality which compels him
to think in ways which the logic of dichotomies denies. We
are summoned to revise fundamentally our ordinary ways of
conceiving experience, and thus, by expanding our vision
and by accepting those forms of thought which also include
nonexclusive categories, the mind is then able to grasp what
it was incapable of grasping or accepting before.

Nature operates out of necessity; there is no alternative in
nature, no will, no freedom, no choice as there is for man.
Man must have convictions and values to live for, and this
also is recognized and accepted by those scientists who are at
the same time philosophers. For they then realize that duty
and devotion to our task, be it a task of acting or of understanding, will become weaker and rarer unless guidance is
sought in a metaphysics that transcends our historical and
scientific views or in a religion that transcends and yet per-
vades the work we are carrying on in the light of day.

For the nature of knowledge, whether scientific or onto-
logical, consists in reconciling *meaning* and *being*. And *being*
signifies nothing other than the actualization of potentiality,
self-realization which keeps in tune with the transformation.
This leads to experience in terms of the individual; and to
organization and patterning in terms of the universe. Thus
organism and world actualize themselves simultaneously.

And so we may conclude that organism is *being* enduring
in time, in fact in eternal time, since it does not have its
beginning with procreation, nor with birth, nor does it end
with death. Energy and matter in whatever form they may
manifest themselves are transtemporal and transspatial and
are therefore metaphysical. Man as man is summoned to
know what is right and what is wrong, for emptied of such
knowledge he is unable to decide what is better or what is
worse.

World Perspectives hopes to show that human society is
different from animal societies, which, having reached a certain stage, are no longer progressive but are dominated by
routine and repetition. Thus man has discovered his own

nature, and with this self-knowledge he has left the state of nonage and entered manhood. For he is the only creature who is able to say not only "no" to life but "yes" and to make for himself a life that is human. In this decision lie his burden and his greatness. For the power of life or death lies not only in the tongue but in man's recently acquired ability to destroy or to create life itself, and therefore he is faced with unlimited and unprecedented choices for good and for evil that dominate our time. Our common concern is the very destiny of the human race. For man has now intervened in the process of evolution, a power not given to the pre-Socratics, nor to Aristotle, nor to the Prophets in the East or the West, nor to Copernicus, nor to Luther, Descartes, or Machiavelli. Judgments of value must henceforth direct technological change, for without such values man is divested of his humanity and of his need to collaborate with the very fabric of the universe in order to bestow meaning, purpose, and dignity upon his existence.

In spite of the infinite obligation of men and in spite of their finite power, in spite of the intransigence of nationalisms, and in spite of the homelessness of moral passions rendered ineffectual by the technological outlook, beneath the apparent turmoil and upheaval of the present, and out of the transformations of this dynamic period with the unfolding of a world-consciousness, the purpose of *World Perspectives* is to help quicken the "unshaken heart of well-rounded truth" and interpret the significant elements of the World Age now taking shape out of the core of that undimmed continuity of the creative proces which restores man to mankind while deepening and enhancing his communion with the universe.

RUTH NANDA ANSHEN

WORLD PERSPECTIVES

Volumes already published.